Running
For Local Office

by Dan Gookin

Running For Local Office For Dummies®

Published by: **John Wiley & Sons, Inc.**, 111 River Street, Hoboken, NJ 07030-5774, www.wiley.com

Copyright © 2019 by John Wiley & Sons, Inc., Hoboken, New Jersey

Published simultaneously in Canada

For general information on our other products and services, please contact our Customer Care Department within the U.S. at 877-762-2974, outside the U.S. at 317-572-3993, or fax 317-572-4002. For technical support, please visit www.wiley.com/techsupport.

Wiley publishes in a variety of print and electronic formats and by print-on-demand. Some material included with standard print versions of this book may not be included in e-books or in print-on-demand. If this book refers to media such as a CD or DVD that is not included in the version you purchased, you may download this material at http://booksupport.wiley.com. For more information about Wiley products, visit www.wiley.com.

Library of Congress Control Number: 2019944099

ISBN: 978-1-119-58817-7; 978-1-119-58822-1 (ebk); 978-1-119-58824-5 (ebk)

Manufactured in the United States of America

C10012187_071719

Contents at a Glance

Table of Contents

Introduction

How did they get elected? That one guy is there to promote his own business. That lady thinks she's better than everyone else. That other lady sleeps half the time. The old guy represents the insiders and back-slappers. That young kid is in way over his head. And the fat guy just can't shut up. Certainly, you can do better!

The desire to enter public service has many motivators. Perhaps you want to do what's right, to direct your energies toward making your community a better place. Maybe you're a reformer, tired of the entrenched status quo, who seem out of touch with the citizens. For whatever reason, you've decided to run for public office. It's an honored American tradition, like opening your own restaurant but with a tremendously higher chance at failure.

About This Book

This book is written to help you make a successful run for public office. It outlines the things that need to be done, what's important, what to avoid, and how to plan and execute a nearly flawless campaign. Nothing is guaranteed, of course, yet this book covers what's necessary to accomplish a successful run — and what to do should things go awry. This text helps get you on your way, outlining the process, from kitchen table conversation to election night victory.

Each chapter covers a topic related to seeking public office. If you want to be successful, you must do more than plant yard signs. Chapters are divided into sections packed with step-by-step details. All the information is cross-referenced, and you can read the book in any order: from front to back or by starting with a topic that intrigues you.

Sample chapter sections include:

>> Understanding who wins elections

>> Building your reputation

>> Cutting short a boring conversation

- » Categorizing your opposition
- » Gathering election data
- » Staging an announcement event
- » Generating name recognition
- » Going door-to-door
- » Dealing with campaign finance problems
- » Avoiding surprises

All topics are fully explained. Nothing is assumed. New terms are clarified as they're introduced. Technical and legal terms are avoided wherever possible. No dreary political history is listed. Finger wagging is at a minimum. Grandstanding, nonexistent.

Foolish Assumptions

This book is specific to running for local office in the United States. *Local office* is defined as an elected position at a political division that isn't statewide. For the most part, these offices include city councils, school districts, and other local boards.

This book does not address running for state legislature, a statewide office such as governor, or any national office. Many of the same techniques written about here apply, but more importantly such positions tend to be partisan. For the most part, local offices are run as nonpartisan elections.

Election laws differ from the state to state. Rules about elections and who can hold office may vary all the way down to the political subdivision where you seek office. Therefore, this book refers to the *election authority,* or the entity that runs the election for the office you seek. It could be a state agency, a county agency, or the agency where you seek office. Regardless, some public entity oversees the election.

Most of the rules regarding a specific public office and the election process are found online, provided by the agency that oversees elections. The agency where you seek office may also publish a candidate's packet, which contains further details. Study the information! Its details are far more specific than what I can offer in this book.

This book doesn't get into partisan politics, nor do I prattle on about the current political divide in this country. My final assumption is that you're a good person who wants to do well for your community. Hopefully, whatever national team you align with doesn't sully your local reputation.

Icons Used in This Book

TIP

This icon flags useful, helpful tips or suggestions.

REMEMBER

This icon marks a friendly reminder to do something.

WARNING

This icon marks a friendly reminder not to do something.

CAMPAIGN
CALENDAR

This icon highlights a date or an event that's useful to put on your master campaign calendar.

DAN
SAYS

This icon flags an aside, an anecdote, or a pithy piece of advice from the author.

Beyond the Book

Bonus information for this title can be found online. You can visit the publisher's website to find an online Cheat Sheet. Go to www.dummies.com and type the book's title, *Running For Local Office For Dummies*, into the Search text box. If the stars are in your favor, you can click the Search button and — behold! — the Cheat Sheet page in the search results list.

Where to Go from Here

Thank you for reading the introduction. Few people bother, so when you make the effort, it makes me feel better. It should make you feel better too, because it shows that you're willing to wade through what many people would consider to be extraneous and boring material — which is exactly what you'll be studying should you get elected.

Your task now is to start reading the rest of the book. You don't need to read the whole thing. My advice is to observe the table of contents and dive into whichever part you feel is important. Or you can read it all in order. Or stop reading after Chapter 3. But read the whole thing; you paid for it.

My email address is dgookin@wambooli.com. That's my real address. I reply to all my email — faster if you keep the message short and to the point. I enjoy saying hi, though I cannot serve as your unpaid campaign advisor, nor do I offer endorsements or make donations. Thank you for understanding.

My website is wambooli.com, where I offer support for all my books, most of which cover technology topics. This book has its own page on my site, where I offer additional information and all sorts of fun stuff. You can find it at

wambooli.com/help/localoffice

Please enjoy the book. I wish you success in your run for local office.

1

Hail, Future Caesar

IN THIS CHAPTER

» **Deciding to be a politician**

» **Understanding election winners**

» **Growing thick skin**

» **Becoming a great candidate**

» **Determining your political type**

» **Dealing with election results**

Chapter **1**

Who Runs for Public Office

An image appears in your head. It's the politician: nice teeth, fabulous hair, smells great, impeccably dressed, infectiously charismatic, popular, smart. Is this you?

No! It's Hollywood. The perfect politician doesn't exist. It's a myth you mustn't let dissuade you from taking a stab at joining the local school board or town council. As you can see from watching these government boards in action, any fool can get elected. Why not take a shot yourself and raise the bar?

To Be a Politician

Have you ever addressed an issue by saying, "If I were king of the universe . . ."? Everyone has an opinion about how things should get done. The position of King of the Universe would be ideal to solve people problems. This position, thankfully, isn't available in our republic.

If your desire is to see things run better, the arena in which you fight is politics.

The word *politics* comes from the Greek πολίτικα *(politika)*, which means "affairs of the city." Politics is often described as "the art of the possible." This phrase means that you can do just about anything, given a rush of money from a spigot that can only open wider.

Before you dive into doing what's right or making things better, ask yourself whether you truly want to become a politician. Is it the best way to reach your goal?

DAN SAYS

>> Politics is not a combination of the words *poly,* meaning "many," and *ticks,* meaning "blood-sucking insects."

>> The "art of the possible" means that politics isn't truly about doing what's right or what's best, but rather about just doing something.

>> The Romans used the term *res publica* for politics. It means "the public thing." It's from this root that we get the word *republic.*

>> Politics is about solving public problems. When no public problems exist, politics is about creating public problems for which no solution exists.

Avoiding public office altogether

It's entirely possible to change the world — or even the policies of the local water district — without being elected. Public pressure is often missing at the local level: Hearings are held and no one shows up, the local press fails to cover the meetings, and officials put little effort into soliciting public input. By your presence alone at a meeting, you effect change. This activism requires no long-term commitment and low public exposure, for the most part.

On the other side of the table, being a politician may seem alluring, but it's also stressful. The job itself is easy enough that any nincompoop who wins an election can hold a guaranteed job for several years. Lack of performance is rarely grounds for dismissal.

No, the stress of being a politician comes from elsewhere. For example, you may feel pressure at work, beyond the routine drama of your regular job. Being away from family, missing out on hobbies, and having an obligation to public service for what's essentially a thankless job can be deflating.

A politician is open to criticism and ridicule, not always justified but always encouraged. You will be teased beyond anything you ever experienced in elementary school, often by people who claim to be adults. On the other hand, if you're a one-issue activist who implores the city council not to demolish that last historic building in town, you may be dismissed by the power players, but that's it. The activist rarely suffers from incessant mockery.

The U.S. election system is built on competition. It's like sports for uncoordinated people: The political spectrum is defined by everyone inside as a struggle between the good guys and the bad guys or, sadly, good-versus-evil. Yes, even at the local level, political life can be nasty.

>> The First Amendment upholds your right to complain about the government. The language is to "petition the government for a redress of grievances." This right covers everything from being abused by government power to being unhappy about a $10 fee to neuter your cat.

>> See Chapter 3 for other ways you can become involved at the local level and effect change.

Understanding who wins elections

For all the talk of who's best-suited for office, an election is really a popularity contest: Popular people win elections. As the current slate of local and national politicians demonstrates, the public doesn't always pick the best or most qualified person for the job.

The typical ballot lacks details about the candidates. On the other hand, a proposition, bond, or levy features detailed language and specifics. For an officeholder, someone who may oversee a multimillion-dollar budget and make decisions that affect tens of thousands of people, the detail is often only a name. Some ballots may show party affiliation, which is rare for local office elections that lack a primary.

>> It's not that the public picks the worst person — it's that the public is conditioned to vote for the lesser of two evils.

>> An election is a marketing campaign. If you want to be the most popular person on the ballot, you must sell yourself. See Part 3.

Having thick skin

Being on the ballot goes beyond a popularity contest. It's personal. If you're going to take the plunge, you must have thick skin. Do you?

Don't discount this question! It's important, especially if your enthusiasm is high and you receive a lot of positive feedback from people encouraging you to run.

Suppose you submit your prized peach pie at the county fair. One of the judges offers that the crust isn't flaky enough. Dashed by receiving only a white ribbon, you withdraw from all social events over the entire summer. If this scenario describes you, you're most likely too sensitive to withstand the slings and arrows of local politics.

Criticism isn't the only needle to pierce thin skin. Your decisions as an elected official are all yes-or-no. You can't cast a maybe vote at the local level. No matter how you vote on a controversial issue, someone is angry, and deservedly so.

Based on your decisions, which you feel are best for the organization or for the public, people you don't know will suddenly hate you. No, they'll despise you. They will project all their hatred upon you, their anger fueled by the mass media and national polarizing politics. This type of disapproval goes beyond that offered by a judge at the county fair (who is getting paid in pie): It's fair criticism. As an elected official, you deserve it.

Is your skin thick enough? You'll find out when you run. Elections are brutal. Brace yourself.

REMEMBER

>> Public officials have a lower bar for slander. In an election, your opponent may accuse you of minor or unspeakable acts that will offend you. In American politics, these accusations are considered fair game.

>> Do you recall ever making a snide comment about a politician? You sneer, "That guy is a scumbag," without knowing him personally or having any details. That's how the public is trained to think of a politician.

>> In a local election, especially a nonpartisan race, extreme criticism is seen as a desperate act. See Chapter 12 for details on how to deal with negative attacks.

>> Criticism can be fair or unfair. It's fair to criticize an elected official for a decision. It's unfair to criticize someone personally, but in our culture, such criticism seems to be routine.

Resisting conformity

I would recommend against running for office if your desire in social settings is to blend in with the group. The weight of social pressure is huge for a politician because most crave acceptance. Human beings are social creatures who value conformity and shun those with different opinions.

As a public official, you must be artful enough to enact change in a manner accepted by people who adore the motto, "We've always done it this way." Groupthink is infectious among elected officials. The river must flow, and no one swims upstream.

If you're the nail that stands up, you must be pounded down. It's extremely uncomfortable to be that nail, especially in an established origination that rewards consensus. Often, freshly elected officials give in to conformity like puppy dogs wanting to belong. That's when they lose focus, abandon their goals, and become part of the problem.

If you're true to your goals when you set out to campaign, resist the urge to change if you win the election and are seated in office.

REMEMBER

>> Having a backbone doesn't mean that you must become philosophically rigid. Always be open to different ideas and willing to change your mind when given new data. The key is to make your own decision and not just echo what the get-along-go-along elected officials have said.

>> The desire to conform is greatest for a local officeholder because your legislative body is so small.

>> If you're successful at resisting conformity, congratulations! You've changed something in government. This success is measurable. One person alone can change an organization through persistence and persuasion.

>> On an elected board, a legislative body, you need more than your own vote to accomplish something. Your persistence pays off when others join you.

>> Some elected bodies are naturally boisterous and no one gets along. In that situation, avoid resisting conformity and instead strive to be the calm voice of reason.

>> Go back and review your election promises. For example, if you promised to hold firm on spending, remind yourself so that you don't submit to peer pressure or the desire of some elected bullies for unanimity.

The Ideal Candidate

Your mental image of the ideal candidate isn't spot-on when it comes to winning elections. After all, compare that image with photos of your crop of local elected officials. Those pictures should be hanging in the post office, yet the lot of them won elections and serve in office. Indeed, whether you're a good fit for public office has little to do with what you look like.

Political parties and activist groups spend a great deal of time searching for the perfect person to run for public office. When they grow desperate, they look for anyone with a pulse. And they fall prey to the curious notion that you must be good-looking to win an election. Being easy-on-the-eyes helps, but it's not everything.

Anyone can run for public office: groomed candidates, regular people wanting to make a difference, and ugly people for pure entertainment. You also find small-minded, sad people attracted to public office because they desire respect they can't otherwise earn in the real world. Don't laugh; a lot of them win.

Truthfully, the ideal candidate doesn't exist. Even your supporters will confide in you, "I don't agree with everything you stand for . . ." The only way you can get someone to truly represent you in office is to run yourself.

TIP

"HE REMEMBERS MY NAME!"

The best politicians remember people's names. The past two governors of my state have both greeted me by saying, "Good to see you again, Dan." I'm floored. You can learn the same trick, which can really boost your appeal as a local candidate.

The key is to repeat someone's name at least three times when you first meet them. You must do it out loud, not in your head.

Your friend: This is my good friend Jerry.

You: Hello, Jerry! It's good to meet you, Jerry. (He won't find it odd that you repeated his name twice.)

Jerry: Blah-blah-blah.

You: That's great, Jerry.

And you're done. You now know Jerry's name forever. The only problem that may cloud your memory is if you're introduced to too many people at once, which makes using this trick more difficult, but not impossible.

To make a difference, strive to become the ideal candidate. This process requires that you study the job, know the voter, and run an excellent campaign. Above all, it's necessary to know yourself. These topics are covered in Part 2.

>> Don't buy into someone saying, "You'd be great on the school board." Unless they are waving a fistful of dollars to fund your campaign or are willing to drive people in a bus to the polling place, don't believe them.

>> Everyone has flaws, the ideal candidate being no exception. If you don't think you have flaws, you haven't looked hard enough.

>> Despair not if you discover that you don't have what it takes. Such news should motivate you to seek out that ideal candidate, support them, and realize the change you seek.

The Political Type

"Oh, I'm not a politician," the politician says. No one likes to think of themselves as being a politician, just as people who sell used cars tell their friends that they sell insurance. Still, I've yet to see someone who doesn't play the political game to some degree.

Running for office makes you a politician. Winning cements it. If you dislike being a politician, stop reading this book now and read *Selling Ice Cream For Dummies*. More people will like you.

Understanding why people run for office

The key reason that good individuals seek public office is to make a difference. They want to be part of the solution. This reason is the best, boldest, most admired reason, yet few of these people ever get elected.

The actual reasons people run for office vary. Even when your goals are pure and you desire to be selfless about the most egotistical thing anyone can do, odds are good that you run for office because

>> You have a single issue that vexes you.

>> You desire to build your résumé.

>> You seek respect and adulation.

>> You want to use the office for some pecuniary benefit.

>> You need membership in higher social circles.

>> You truly want to be King of the Universe someday.

Don't let any of these items offend you. Sonny Bono ran for mayor in Palm Springs because he was frustrated with City Hall. He won and served well, addressing matters beyond the one that motivated him to get into the race. For many others, however, this list describes the underlying reason that a run for public office is an itch to scratch.

You may not admit it publicly, but if your reason is on this list, or perhaps is more targeted but still something you wouldn't share in your campaign material, fine. Should you be elected, you may find that realizing such a goal isn't the solution to your problems.

Part 4 of this book offers recommendations for those who win an election.

Becoming one of them

I believe that all elected officials start their terms in office with positive enthusiasm, respect for their organization, and a desire to do well. Whatever infects them afterward manifests itself in three ways. These three categories classify the different types of elected official, according to my observations:

>> **Self-promoters:** These people have a top desire to promote themselves or their businesses. They may seek inside information to expand their real estate empires or those of their friends, direct business toward themselves or their friends, or engage in other scurrilous acts. I'm not making this up! Check out the ethics-in-government laws for your state and you'll see that these aren't original ideas — nor do the ethics laws stanch the self-promoters and their specific interests.

The benefit can also be personal: A self-promoter uses political office to gain entry to clubs, get special treatment or favors, and find other ways to cut in line before the people they represent.

>> **The clueless:** This type of elected official is the most common, despite the first category getting the most attention. Making government decisions requires that you be a quick study. Your job wanders between issues of public concern to staff-pushed issues to funding to strange legal concepts you never heard of before and more. Not everyone is equipped to handle such an information overload, so the clueless ignore everything and vote with the crowd.

>> **Boy scouts:** I admire elected officials who consistently try to do what's right. They aren't always successful, but they're persistent. Trust me: You will be admired for taking a stand when you believe in something, especially when your decision offers no specific benefit to yourself. This is the type of elected official I believe the public wants, and the type you should strive to become.

Almost everyone takes office assuming that they're going to behave like a Boy Scout, admired and praised for always doing the right thing. That praise may never come. Still, keep on track and do what's right. As best you can, try to avoid becoming a self-promoter. These are the political types the public loathes and distrusts.

>> Alas, even those politicians who violate ethics laws get reelected. You can change that by running against them. See Chapter 6.

>> One reason so many local elected officials are clueless is that they suffer no immediate consequences for not doing the job. Unlike in school, no one marks you down for not reading the engineer's report on irrigation pipe sizes and flow rates. Keep your mouth shut and vote with the majority and no one will ever know.

TIP

>> Your campaign promises become a message to your future self, reminding an elected official what a constituent such as yourself really wants.

Accept the Results

Not everyone who runs for office wins, which is something any of the dozens of living people who've run for president can vouch for. The person who comes in first with the most votes is the winner. Everyone else in the election, no matter how close, goes home without any lovely parting gifts.

What the public ends up with isn't the best person for the office, but rather the best candidate. That's the system. Therefore, if you desire to be a good elected official, you must be a good candidate. This is the first step.

The second step to winning an election is to run as nearly a flawless campaign as you can. Because political campaigns are newsworthy, you probably have a notion of how they work. As in any marketing campaign, the key to success is not to spend money and waste resources foolishly. Even experienced politicians have trouble with this step.

Finally, the last step is to accept the results. If you did poorly, consider another alternative to being elected. Chapter 3 offers options.

If you did well, consider running again. Keep your attitude sunshine-positive, and keep fighting for what you believe in. Stay active. Above all, avoid attacking the winner or degrading the system. Lots of politicians lose races and win again because they're positive and persistent.

The worst thing that can happen is that you win. Being an elected official is the goal, but it comes with some interesting restrictions. Don't forget the people who put you in office, as well as all the people you represent, and pray that you serve them well in your new role.

>> Don't despair if you lose. The only true losers are those who never try.

>> If you made a good attempt, give yourself credit for shaping the debate.

>> Ability has nothing to do with who wins an election. Voters have made some terrible choices, as the country's history can attest.

>> For partisan elections, voter affiliation has more power than a candidate's character.

>> If you lose, recognize that the timing may not be right. Consider your election effort as establishing yourself, your name, your credibility. Do better the next time and your goal will be realized.

>> See Part 4 for details on what to expect should the horrible thing happen and you win the election.

Chapter **2**

Local Office Choices

I f your passion leads to you a specific local office, great! But don't let those high-visibility offices, such as school district or city council, detract you from other ways of serving your community. Many boards and commissions need quality leadership. Don't believe that your options are limited.

Political Hierarchy

If you fear that the country has too much government, you're correct. Yet the structure is more efficient than if a single bloated entity tried to handle everything. In fact, you may be surprised to discover that your residence's location, which is used for voting and taxing purposes, is affected by dozens of government entities, each of which has a specific role.

These jurisdictions are called *political divisions.* They blanket and overlap the country, providing various services and offering multiple frustrations to their respective populations. Each political division has an elected board, though some have boards appointed by other elected officials.

Figure 2-1 illustrates a generic map of the political divisions in the United States. Here are how these divisions work:

>> **Federal:** At the top level is the national government, "the Fed," named after the federal government. The Fed is the country's second attempt at a national government, after the Confederation failed. Otherwise, "the Feds" would be called "the Confeds."

>> **State:** After Uncle Fed comes the first major political division in the US: state government. The country is divided into 50 states, each of which boasts that it excels at something and laments that it ranks 50th at something else.

Both the Feds and the states have elected officials, though this level of office seeker isn't covered in this book. If your desire is to seek higher office, I recommend the book *Selling Your Soul For Dummies*.

>> **County:** Within each state, the next level of political division is the county. You can see patchwork quilt boundaries on a map — some square and some resembling a Rorschach test.

Not every state has counties. In Alaska, this division is called a *borough,* and in Louisiana it's a *parish*. Rhode Island did away with counties in 1846. Connecticut abolished the county level of government in 1960. Other states would like to abolish county government or just rename it to keep the public guessing.

>> **Regional:** This large political division rides over county lines as a regional government. For example, a school district may straddle two or more counties. Water and irrigation districts, fire protection districts, and others may also cover more than a single county.

>> **City:** Within counties you find the next major political division, the municipality or municipal corporation. These come in several varieties: city, town, village, borough, and other terms usually dependent on the municipality's population or physical size. They're all cities, as far as this book is concerned.

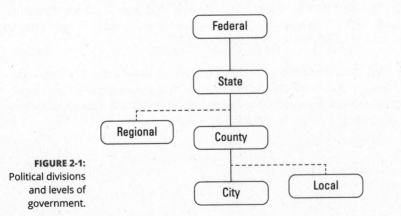

FIGURE 2-1:
Political divisions and levels of government.

A municipality may be further divided into wards or precincts, which are generally the smallest political divisions.

>> **Local:** Other political divisions may be limited to counties, such as hospital districts, environmental districts, and other services. These differ from the regional political divisions in that they exist only within the county.

Each of these political divisions sports a team of elected officials who fill administrative or policy-making roles. And when they screw up, they provide a source of entertainment for the locals. The good news is that elections are held at regular intervals, so the current cast of clowns is exchanged for a new set every so often.

The names for elected officials vary, depending on the area's history, tradition, and lack of non-offensive terms that would otherwise be used. These names include the city council, board of selectmen, aldermen, and so on. The county elected officials might be commissioners or supervisors. School districts generally have trustees, which is a term that could be applied to other elected boards as well.

Local Office Options

When you register to vote, you supply a residence address and a mailing address. Often both are the same, but the reason for the difference is that your residence, the location where you live, is affected by various political divisions. The divisions provide you services, charge you taxes, and allow you to vote for representation on their boards.

>> Your residency determines your status as an *elector,* which is a person who has the right to vote in an election.

>> Only electors in a given political division can run for public office in that division.

DAN SAYS

>> It may surprise you to discover how many elected positions are available to you at the local level. For example, for my residence I have 3 county commissioners, 6 other elected county positions (sheriff, clerk, treasurer, and so on), 6 members of the city council plus 1 mayor, 5 hospital district trustees, 3 highway district commissioners, 1 school district trustee (by zone), and 1 community college trustee (by zone). That's 26 elected local positions.

Exploring political divisions

Some of the political divisions in which you can serve as an elected official are obvious because they're part of our culture. The two that bubble to the top of the list are your local school district and city council.

For a wider scope, you can consider a county office. A county position is still local, though it may be a partisan office — and if your county teems with people, it could be a substantial election effort to attain office.

Beyond the well-known offices, you find low-interest positions that don't frequently make the news. These political divisions deal with specific services, such as water and sewer. The job may be routine, but if the law requires public representation to oversee tax dollars, an election is held for the public to choose the board.

>> Not everyone lives within a city, but everyone does live in a school district.

>> See the later section "Knowing your taxing districts" to discover how many potential elected positions are available to you.

Selecting a seat

Choosing to run for a specific office may involve a secondary decision, such as which seat to occupy. This decision has nothing to do with which chair you sit in after you win. Instead, it deals with how the government body divides its region — or not.

For example, some political divisions classify their elected officials by seat. Some split their territory into zones. The reason for doing so is to ensure adequate and fair representation throughout the district. This split affects the composition of the government board in different ways, as reflected by how you run for the position. Here are the options:

>> **At large:** For this elected position, your name goes on the ballot with a group of people. Also called a *horse race,* its top vote-getters are the ones who take office. As an example, when three seats are up for election and five people are running, only the top three vote-getters take office.

>> **By seat:** For some elected positions, you must specify a seat. For example, seats 1, 3, and 5 on the library board are up for election. You choose a seat to run for and then enter that race with others for the same seat. These seats aren't tied to a specific district or zone, though they can be.

>> **By zone:** Larger political districts are often split into zones, typically to ensure equitable representation throughout the area. When seeking this office, you must run for the zone or district in which you reside.

Some of these options may be combined. For example, a hospital district may have four zones but also one official who is elected at large, meaning they can live anywhere and run for that seat.

> >> Depending on the election laws in your state, only those who live in a specific zone may be allowed to vote for representatives from that zone. It may also be true that everyone within the district votes, but those who run can only be from specific zones.
>
> >> Winning an election by seat doesn't necessarily tie into where you sit during a meeting. The word *seat* refers to the office, not a chair.
>
> >> Also see Chapter 8 for more information on selecting how to run for a position.

Knowing your taxing districts

For the most part, elected officials in the United States oversee the spending of public money. Their political divisions are also taxing districts. These officials serve many roles, chief of which is to represent the public in governmental matters as well as oversee the spending of public money.

One quick way to discover which districts affect you, and therefore which you're eligible to run for, is to look at your tax and utility bills.

Your tax bill lists those agencies authorized to levy taxes, such as income or property taxes. Each line item on the bill is associated with a political division that most likely is run by a cohort of elected officials.

Likewise, your utility bills may feature political divisions, such as water or sewer districts. These organizations could be private firms serving as government sanctioned monopolies, but they could also be government entities. Often, a public board oversees such utilities.

The tax or utility bill may have additional information you can check to further research elected positions available to you. But also see the later section "Letting the office find you" for good advice on how to choose an elected position.

TIP

> >> Some taxing districts may have appointed officials. Usually an elected official makes the appointments, such as a governor appointing a district board, which may happen with the approval of the legislature.
>
> >> Check your city or county's website to look for mapping or GIS (geographic information system) software. These clever programs can help you discover which taxing districts affect your residence.

Choose an Office

You probably know someone who runs in every election — the same name continually seeking an elected position. He runs for county commissioner, loses. He runs for sheriff, loses. He runs for school board, loses. He's the perennial candidate, running to sate his own ego as opposed to seeking to contribute. You don't want to be that guy.

Letting the office find you

The best way to run for office is to let the office find you. You've been showing up at the meetings or watching on TV. You know the players. You understand the issues. In that case, the office is calling you. Easy choice.

The office can also call you in other ways: You're frustrated with a zone change. The school board selected a new firm to supply computers, and that firm is owned by the chairman's brother. The public ambulance service takes too long to get to your part of the county. The water district keeps raising rates, and not one trustee questions the increases. These are many of the reasons that drive people to a specific public office.

DAN SAYS

Informed voters can tell when a candidate has a passion for the office. Alas, most people who vote are uninformed.

Making a good fit

Just because you find yourself attracted to a specific office may not mean that you're a good fit. It's important to judge your experience versus your desire to serve. Ask yourself, what are you good at?

As an example, successful business owners may excel in administrative positions, such as mayor or county clerk, as opposed to legislative positions, such as school district trustee or city council member. This notion doesn't rule out running for one type of position or another, but you should understand how you can best focus your strengths in your public service.

>> Among other important factors to consider are your existing obligations. Though some elected officials phone it in, if you plan on doing actual work for your community, you must devote time to the job. If you have a heavy workload or are out of town frequently or if your schedule is inflexible, you might consider other ways of contributing, as described in Chapter 3.

» Filling an administrative position means that you direct other people (non-elected staff). The decisions you make are according to the laws, rules, and policies of the organization.

» A legislative position deals with setting policy. The policy directs staff and administration. In a legislative position — council member, selectman, trustee — you can craft policy and set direction only when acting in a group. You cannot order staff around as an individual.

» Pay and benefits are other considerations for making a good fit with public office. Even so, it's never considered admirable to run for office because you need a paycheck.

Partisan Effects

Consider yourself fortunate if the local office you seek is nonpartisan and otherwise free from the political dividing line of R and D. Still, the dank shadow of partisan politics may cast itself upon the office you seek. It changes the entire game.

Running along party lines

Occasionally, for whatever reason, a local office is partisan. Beyond national political baggage entering the race, the effect is that the election has both primary and general phases. You must be successful in the primary to win your party's nomination, and then you must win the general election to take office.

To win a partisan race, it's best to run as a partisan. This requirement means you must declare for one party or the other, even when you detest them both.

People choose a political party for whatever reason — some out of personal belief, family tradition, or loyalty. Others choose it out of convenience: In those states where one party dominates, a clever politician associates with the majority party regardless of his or her convictions. The goal is to get elected, right?

TIP

One way to ensure your partisan *bone fides* is to be involved with the party. The social elite of either party like people they know or who come highly recommended. It also helps to attend the annual fundraiser — Jefferson–Jackson Day for the Democrats or Lincoln Day for the Republicans — and participate in the meetings, picnics, and other social events.

If you don't have time to attend the party's social events, money talks. Heavy dona-tors to political parties (not to specific candidates) curry favor with party people.

>> The name of the annual fundraiser can change from state to state. For example, Republicans may have a Lincoln-Reagan Day dinner. The Democrats may hold a Unity Dinner. The names of locally famous politicians may also be included in the fundraiser's name.

>> Nonpartisan local races are more about old money than party politics.

>> I ran in a partisan race as an independent and got my clock cleaned. People are conditioned to vote the party line in the general election. Yet the silly thing is that many partisans told me they would have preferred to vote for me had I run as a member of their party.

DAN
SAYS

Avoiding partisan politics

Even in a nonpartisan local race, pressure mounts for candidates to declare one way or another. It's not that the position has anything to do with partisan politics, but years of training has convinced voters that declaring one way or the other somehow matters.

Most local decisions have little to do with the major national issues that divide people. Further, it's rare that a party platform addresses local issues. Yet the par-tisan influence can be strong, thanks to the media and to party loyalists who value the D or the R above honesty and character.

I would caution you not to thrust partisanship into a nonpartisan race. The only positive aspect I can think of is that in regions where the demographic leans strongly in one direction, partisan politics may have an influence. In a general sense, it shows how you stand on issues such the role of government in people's lives.

>> One issue you will encounter, especially when going door-to-door, is that people will ask for your party affiliation. I recommend that you fess up but also explain that it's a nonpartisan race.

>> Sometimes, identifying as a partisan in a nonpartisan race annoys people. Many voters prefer that local politics remain free of the divisiveness that infects national politics. Coming out strongly partisan in a nonpartisan race, such as putting your party affiliation on campaign materials, can backfire.

>> Avoid bringing national issues into a local race, especially if they have no relevance to the position. Only if the government body is already debating or has considered an issue that has national relevance, should you inject a divisive national issue into a local race to appeal to a partisan crowd.

WARNING

Chapter **3**

Other Ways to Get Involved

Not every road to political success ends with holding office. In fact, many of the most powerful people in your town most likely aren't elected officials. Instead, they have those elected officials do their bidding. These people can get their way, and it's perfectly legal, without being elected simply by wielding their influence.

On the fringes, people with single issues and a full tank of determination can also effect change without suffering through a campaign and experiencing the agony of occupying elected office. They can be active in other ways, chair committees, or organize groups of citizens. They may not be elected, but they can initiate change.

Boost Your Public Résumé

Having a brilliant idea is worthless. The people who succeed are those who put in effort to promote the idea. Money helps. But in the realm of politics, what you really need in order to succeed — whether you choose to run or stay on the sidelines — is a glowing public résumé.

Building your reputation

No one records their public involvement as they would write a résumé or *curriculum vitae*. The reputation you build is a public one, and success is measured by people who can vouch for you, your dedication, and your behavior.

Ninety percent of success is showing up. To build your public reputation, you must show up to meetings. Attend functions related to the topics that interest you. Scour the legal notices in the local paper; most jurisdictions are required to provide public notice in a newspaper or a meeting — hopefully, with an agenda. If not, look online for meeting notices and agendas.

Attending meetings means you must tolerate being able to sit for long periods. I'm serious: You must build your stamina to not only sit still but also feign interest in whatever topic is presented. Public meetings are vacuums of intelligent thought and deserts of lively discourse. You must increase your tolerance levels. If you become elected, get used to drawn-out meetings and people pretending to be experts on various dull topics.

Above all, be polite and respectful. If you're given the opportunity for input, always say something positive. It's true that you're trying to help. Even when you dislike something, frame it in a positive way. Avoid colorful language and don't exaggerate, no matter how much it entertains you.

DAN SAYS

» A concerning issue at public meetings is signing in. In some states, it's illegal to sign in or identity yourself at a public meeting. The idea is that you have a right to address a government body without fear of retribution. Even when sign-up sheets are presented, signing them is optional.

» When visibility isn't important, watch public meetings that are broadcast on PEG (public/educational/governmental) cable channels or on the Internet. A benefit of watching meetings recorded on the Web is that you can increase the watching speed, which helps elected officials and others get their point across without sucking all the air from the room.

» From personal experience, I can tell you that it's difficult to build a reputation when the powers that be actively work against you. Don't let their anger thwart you! Be persistent. Be factual. Be even more visible. Eventually the public recognizes who's telling the truth.

Becoming a community leader

After you've built a public reputation, and people know you and what you stand for, the next step is to become a community leader. This is a position others must give you. Like becoming King of France, you just can't announce that you hold the title of community leader. No one will believe you.

After attending meetings and getting to know people on the committees, turn in an application. It's much easier to be accepted when other members can vouch for you. It's not that attending the meetings beforehand is required, but it increases the odds that you'll be nominated to serve.

Beyond government committees, build your public résumé by joining service groups and nonprofit boards. This role requires that you dedicate your time and write checks, which is great if you believe in the service club's or nonprofit's mission. Your goal is to have even more people vouch for you.

>> Avoid joining too many committees at once to artificially boost your reputation. Don't overextend yourself, which is a negative mark. Good people are appreciated the most when they can dedicate a chunk of their time and attention to a cause.

>> Having a good record of providing community service and occupying leadership positions on various boards provides for great campaign material. See Chapter 9.

The Activist and the Gadfly

Two types of people operate outside of the government realm, both of which can effect change in different ways. They are the activist and the gadfly. These terms represent different approaches to solving public policy issues. The differences between them are subtle, though *gadfly* is a dismissive term and *activist* is an admired one.

Underestimating the gadfly

If you're called a *gadfly* by an elected official, it means that whatever you're doing is working. They use the term dismissively, but if you weren't having an effect, they wouldn't otherwise notice. *Gadfly* isn't necessarily a negative term.

Typically, a gadfly is an upset citizen who has a single issue. They often don't back down when fighting the beast. Elected officials who ignore them only invigorate the gadfly's resolve.

The hallmark of the gadfly is that once the issue is resolved, they go away. Otherwise, they continue to bite and sting until the agency acknowledges the problem. Astute elected officials deftly handle gadflies; poor elected officials create an incubator in which the gadfly thrives.

>> To avoid being gadfly, ensure that your criticism is coupled with suggestions for improvement.

>> The most successful gadflies I know don't mind the label. Sadly, they're in the game to have fun and annoy people.

>> The term *gadfly* describes a type of insect that bites cattle or other livestock. It's a pest. I find that elected officials who apply the term to members of the public are unable to handle dissent.

Becoming an activist

An *activist* is merely a different type of gadfly, one who remains positive and therefore sees success across multiple issues. Complaining while being positive is an art form.

An activist can be focused on a single issue or cover a variety of issues, usually couched in a specific cause: a neighborhood, government transparency, public rights, raising taxes, and other political topics. They take great pains to prove their case and promote their cause in a positive way.

One great difference I've seen from activists who wouldn't be labeled as gadflies is that they're willing to meet with officials one-on-one. They don't use a public meeting to grandstand or promote themselves. The personal meetings help build a reputation, which results in positive movement on an issue.

Here are some tips for becoming a successful activist:

>> Be consistent with your message and delivery. Stay focused.

>> Be positive.

>> Always offer one or more solutions to the problem presented.

>> If you meet with an elected official in private, remind them of that during a public meeting. Especially when they prove to be defensive or evasive, showing that you've met in private demonstrates to the public that you tried.

>> Speak at public meetings. Prepare your speech. Time it to 30 seconds less than the time allotted. Be concise. State facts.

>> Write letters to the editor that focus on your issue and your suggested solutions. Encourage other citizens to assist you.

>> Don't be put off by an entrenched status quo. The "we've always done it this way" cohort can be defeated with persistence, logic, and a positive attitude.

Joining a party

Your typical activist or gadfly is labeled as such because they lack a multitude of voices behind them, cheering the cause. One way to gather those voices is to join and be active in a political party. This move doesn't guarantee that you'll get everyone in the party to agree with you, but it's a healthy step toward gathering momentum.

Be aware that most local issues are not partisan in nature. Local political parties may reject taking a stand on a local issue, which is preferred. What you're after is support from party members, which is easier to find in a group of like-minded people, even if the issue isn't related to a plank in the party platform.

As with any organization, don't expect to show up one day and get followers agreeing with your cause. You must spend time in the trenches and be a good party loyalist to gather any clout. Once you've proven yourself, it's easier to find people willing to rally to your cause than it is as a lone wolf.

The only caution I can offer is that it's dangerous in our current divisive political climate to politicize a local issue that is nonpartisan by nature. When you do so, you bring the national divide to a local issue. For example, you may find that both Democrats and Republicans are opposed to the new asphalt plant. If you rally the troops of one party against the plan, you may find that the other party opposes you simply because they're trained to do so.

>> Local issues are nonpartisan by nature, which is why so many local offices are nonpartisan.

>> As in any social club, members of a political party can be good workers who will help you advance your cause, but they can also be back-stabbing jerks. I know a lot of people who've left a political party frustrated because of personal politics taking a priority over implementing good public policy.

>> Being a recognized member of a party can help you gain support should you choose to run for public office later. Even in a nonpartisan race, the endorsement of or financial support from current and former elected officials carries weight, particularly if you or the office you seek aren't familiar to voters.

Stay Behind the Curtain

Call them the power brokers or the kingmakers, key people hold sway over many important decisions made locally. They do so behind the scenes or out in the open, but they do it without holding public office. I classify these people as powerful or influential. It's possible to be both.

Knowing the power players

If you read the local paper or follow the online community gossip blogs, you probably know the power players: business owners, bankers, developers, current and former officeholders, and other names prominent in your community. These people often hold the reigns of power without holding elected office. They're behind many of the more curious decisions made in government.

Power players rely on their money but also their family name as the foundation of their control. Many of the battles that take place in small jurisdictions have more to do with historic rivalries than with common sense or what's good for the public. The power players are in the thick of these entanglements, which naturally leech into local government.

The true power player doesn't start out wanting to hold elected office. They may recognize that they have no hope of winning political office or are otherwise too busy. Even so, such a step isn't necessary because they can get things done through their power and intimidation. Such results aren't possible when you lack money or a family name.

REMEMBER

>> If you're a candidate, be wary of tightly aligning with a power player. Such support can have an advantage, but you can also lose support through the same association.

>> Power players often gain their position through fear and intimidation.

>> Power players have higher exposure than influential people. This exposure comes from their family name or money, or both. Don't believe anyone who claims to be a power player but lacks the name or the cash.

Becoming an influential person

The problem with being a power player is exposure. Some of them like the attention. Other important people in town, including people without family names and money, desire a lower exposure. These are people of influence.

Influential people know other people. They're trustworthy. They don't seek the spotlight or press their weight to get their way publicly. Instead, they operate behind the scenes effectively and quietly. A word in confidence from them spreads widely and with the same impact and effect as a power player. These are the true kingmakers.

If it's your desire to be a person of influence, you must earn a solid reputation as someone trustworthy. Start by working for a candidate. Volunteer. Meet other people who are politically active and listen to them. Always be honest. Use the experience you accumulate and inside political knowledge to offer frank advice to those who ask.

You have a better chance of being a person of influence over being a power player. It's a more desirable position than being a high-exposure power player, and it's more valuable to others who seek public office.

>> You know you've become a person of influence when others ask you whom to vote for or seek your opinion on a government matter.

>> Influential people shy away from public endorsements. Their value lies in connections with other important people, those who may go public or tell their friends whom to support.

>> Gossips trade in rumors and innuendo. They are not influential people in that they can't be trusted to relay the truth. A true influential person knows the rumors but chooses not to share them unless asked.

2

Before You Run

Chapter **4**

Know Yourself

As a kid, I figured that if Mary Poppins could use an umbrella to fly, so could I. The only thing that kept me from jumping from the garage roof was that I knew I was fat. I required a larger umbrella.

When you float into the political arena, ensure that you know how large of an umbrella you need. The key to gauging its size is to know yourself. This question isn't as philosophical as it is brutally honest.

Some Vital Questions

You may think you know yourself. Great. You trust that you'll be an excellent candidate. Outstanding. Confirm your knowledge by asking some vital questions. Ask these questions to yourself but also to people you trust.

Asking family and friends

Your desire to seek public office shouldn't come as a surprise to the people closest to you. The decision involves these people because you need their support. If you don't have it, you must seriously consider whether being an elected official is the best route for you to take.

Specifically, before you take any step in the direction of running for office, talk with your spouse. Ensure that you have your partner's full, enthusiastic support. Discuss your desire with close members of your family. The race also affects them in that you'll be occupied with a campaign and potentially taking office; you won't be available to them as you normally are.

Determine whether your friends support the move. Get them to be as honest as possible, and truly listen to their reactions. They see you in a different light than your family does, so their opinions will differ.

>> Unlike in a high-profile election, your family, friends, and associates won't be scrutinized by your opponents and the media during a local election.

>> The opinions of your friends and family are valuable. Don't discount their input, because their friends, coworkers, and extended families will be asking about you. Knowing what they think in advance is vital to presenting yourself as a good candidate.

Knowing your public exposure

A local election is all about name recognition. The more the public recognizes a name, the better the chances that name wins. Especially for a local, nonpartisan race, public exposure is the key to winning.

An engaged citizen must have an inkling of who you are to be interested in voting for you. Yes, campaign material can educate them, but if you already have a high public exposure, you get a leg up.

Public exposure also works in the other direction: Do you know the public? You need not memorize the name of everyone in a political district, but it's important that you recognize some key players. If you must ask yourself who the key players are, you're not ready to run; your public exposure is too low.

REMEMBER

Remember that the word *exposure* means something. Ask yourself whether you're comfortable being in public. Do you enjoy speaking to a crowd? Do you mind if people talk about you when you're not there, say things about you that may not be true, or criticize you? You can grow thick skin over time, but if you don't enjoy the exposure, don't run.

TIP

>> Having low public exposure doesn't necessarily exclude you from winning, but it diminishes your chances considerably.

>> If someone introduces you to an influential person and you don't know them, you're not ready to run.

>> Public exposure is one reason why incumbents can so easily win reelection. People recognize their names from the paper, from attending meetings, and from interacting with government.

>> Alas, for a partisan race, the key to winning is really the number of Democrats or Republicans in the district. Many odious candidates have won office based on party affiliation over their character.

>> For a partisan race, name recognition counts most in the primary.

Discovering your abilities

After observing elected officials at the local level, and being one myself, I can tell you that no special skills, talent, or intelligence are required in order to serve. It helps. It's welcome when it happens. Yet it's rare. As far as your abilities, you already have what it takes to do the job.

What helps is understanding how meetings run. Specifically, it's good to have experience participating in meetings hosted by service groups, volunteer organizations, social clubs, church groups, and so on. These meetings run differently from business meetings you might already be familiar with.

A big plus is serving on a board or being the chair or president of an organization. Such experience is good for your public exposure and also demonstrates to others that you can be effective in a legislative structure.

>> To be an effective elected official, you must be effective in a group. Rare is the swaggering grandstander who sees a second term in office.

>> Yes, it's difficult to get work done in a group. Public policy making is slow and cumbersome for a reason: The public's business must take place in public.

Reaching your goal

Before you tackle an endeavor like holding a public position, ensure that you have solid goals in mind. Even if your goal is to get invited to the best football parties, it's a goal. Have that goal and ensure you reach it.

Your goal will help you craft a good campaign. Knowing it also helps you answer questions asked on the campaign trail. A strong, focused goal — even if it isn't entirely true — is necessary.

DAN SAYS

>> Be honest about your goal. If you're running because City Hall is narrowing your street and it will hurt your business, let the people know! Odd as it seems, the voting public values honesty.

>> I don't like small-minded people wanting to hold office because they want to be big shots, yet the public seems to elect them in abundance.

FINE GOALS TO HAVE WHEN RUNNING FOR OFFICE

I want to restore transparency in government.

I speak for those who have been shut out of the system.

I'm tired of the good ol' boys running things.

We need someone who can ask questions.

I won't be a rubber stamp for the [developers, entrenched bureaucrats — pick your bad guys].

Someone must fight for fiscal responsibility and lower taxes.

I want to ask the common sense questions no one asks.

They need to stop ignoring people from my part of town.

TERRIBLE GOALS TO HAVE WHEN RUNNING FOR OFFICE

I've been crapped on all my life, and now it's my turn.

Winning this office will help drive customers to my business.

I want all the freebies that come with being an elected official.

Elected officials are drunks, and my husband owns a liquor store.

I know these guys are getting kickbacks, and I want some action, too.

I want to know where they'll be buying property next so that I can get in on the action.

I'm doing this so that my kids can finally get on the high school honor roll.

This is only the first step because in four years I will be a US Senator.

I'm doing this for the dark lord Moloch.

Explore Your Past

Gone are the days when those silly things you did as a teenager or college student would be forgotten in the mist of time. Hazy memory or not, when you run for office, your past is open for exploration. It's *National Enquirer* exploration, too, not *National Geographic*.

It's important that you review your history — specifically, the ugly parts. You must be ready to deal with things you may have done once but never thought would matter. Explore your past, because your opponent will.

Remembering what you've done

Your personal, private, and public history becomes an open book when you run for office. As a candidate, you're no longer shielded from exposure to prior indiscretions. Though none of these incidents may come to light during a campaign, still you must remember what you've done so that you can prepare a defense.

What skeletons do you have in your closet? Seriously, you must confess them to yourself, but also to your family and associates. Your campaign staff should know as well.

Here are the nasty questions:

>> Have you ever been arrested?

>> Have you had a DUI?

>> Is a domestic violence charge on your public record?

>> Have you ever employed an undocumented worker?

>> Do you pay taxes on household employees?

>> Have you ever declared bankruptcy?

>> Are you behind on your taxes?

A positive answer to any of these questions can be career-ending for a public official. And keep in mind that most of these items are part of your public record. Anyone can look them up.

The key to dealing with these items is to prepare should one or more come out as an issue during a campaign. You'd better have a smart and effective way to deal with them if they arise.

Beyond your public record, you also have a trail on the Internet. That cute picture of you acting inappropriately on your holiday in Cabo may have been hilarious on Facebook years ago, but now it becomes your opponent's chief campaign photo of you. The Internet is written in ink. And, yes, they can tell when you go on an image purge. Someone may have a copy.

People have long memories. Did you get into a fender bender and scream at the kid driving the other car? That may come out. Denying it will hurt you, so remember it now and deal with it should it come up.

The point of remembering what you did isn't to make you feel bad. Everyone has past incidents that they regret or wish had happened in a different way. For a political campaign, however, knowing these items beforehand helps you defend against them. It also may help you determine that you have too much baggage and that therefore it would be better for you to remain behind the scenes rather than run for office.

>> Exposing your past is fair game in a campaign. Your opponents will examine your criminal history, including speeding tickets, divorce records, failure to pay taxes — all of it.

>> Don't fret: Your campaign must do a background check on your opponent as well. See Chapter 6.

Dealing with potential issues

When your skeletons present and past are known and exposed, the next step is discussing how to deal with them. Above all, you must never deny that something took place.

Come clean when confronted with an issue. Admit it. Because you've already reviewed your past — and reviewed it with family, friends, associates, and campaign staff — you're ready to deal with the issue in a calm and logical way.

The worst thing to do is lie. Lying about something you did increases its magnitude by several degrees in the negative direction. For example, if you didn't pay your taxes and you lie about it, you've just given your opponent campaign gold. You've also cast doubt in the eyes of your supporters. If instead you admit to the deed and follow up with a calm explanation, you might gain respect; everyone has misfortune.

The best news is that you need not confess to anything that doesn't come up. Don't open the debate by saying, "I did a lot of drugs." If it comes up, deal with it because you've reviewed your past and you're ready. Otherwise, don't disclose.

>> Sad to say, if you lie about something you did, your public reputation cannot be restored. Even sadder is that incumbents can get away with such behavior and the voters don't seem to care.

>> Don't worry: In a political campaign, people you don't know will dislike you for whatever little reason. To paraphrase Steve Jobs, if you want everyone to like you, sell ice cream.*

>> Also see Chapter 6 for information on a SWOT analysis, which can help you deal with weaknesses in your campaign as well as your opponent's.

---

* "If you want to make everyone happy, don't be a leader, sell ice cream."
– Steve Jobs.

Sell Yourself

A political campaign is a marketing endeavor. The product you're selling is yourself. You've probably never been a product before, so the notion of having to sell yourself is a strange concept. If it's difficult, you hire competent people to help you. On your own, as part of knowing yourself, you must be able to do a few minor things to improve your public character.

>> Realtors, car dealers, and lawyers market themselves, which is probably one reason so many of them run for office.

>> Does selling yourself make you a whore? Indeed it does! Politics is only one notch removed from the world's oldest profession.

>> Stop feeling dirty. People support you because they believe in you and want you to do well in office. You need not sell your soul or reputation to climb the political ladder. In fact, you might be that rare elected official who brings respect to the position. To get there, you must sell yourself.

Believing you can do it

When you see a good politician in action, observe how confident they are. Even when they're wrong or you disagree with them 100 percent, they have a poise and confidence that expresses how strongly they believe in what they're saying. Wishy-washy people seldom succeed in politics.

Fill the room with your buoyancy and positive attitude. Believe in what you're selling, yourself. Have answers for questions. Be eager to meet people. Act like you're having the most fun doing the best thing that anyone in the world could be doing at that moment.

>> Candidates with low confidence pass it along like an infection.

>> Refer to the earlier section "Reaching your goal," for information on keeping a goal during your campaign. Focus on that goal as one of the key concepts you believe in.

>> Smile in public.

>> People admire solid answers to questions. When you don't know the answer, tell them you'll get back with an answer soon. Self-confidence is important to your success, even when you make up crap.

>> During one campaign, I knew I was going to lose. I was privy to private polling information that showed me way behind. Despite the dismal data, I kept my attitude positive in public. When people asked, I told them I felt great and thought I would do well. I didn't lie, but I didn't pass on the depressing news.

Acting the part

A candidate for office must be a very public person. Successful politicians know how to deal with people, know what's expected of them in public, and know how to act the part.

Learn to work the room. This tactic means you enter a space with people and speak with as many as you can. Stop by and say hello to people you know, but also walk up to people you don't and introduce yourself: "I'm Erin Smith, candidate for Highland Irrigation District Seat 2." Just do it.

When you meet someone, shake their hand. Make eye contact when you do. Smile. It *is* great to meet them, a voter. Maintain eye contact until they break it, which is generally right away.

Practice your small talk. See the later sidebar, "Small-talk tips." The key isn't knowing what to say as much as when to stop and move on. You don't want to spend too much time with someone when your goal is to work the room.

REMEMBER

Assume you're being observed. Yes, the cocktail waitress may be the most attractive woman you've ever seen, but don't flirt. She's a voter, too, and your opponent's supporters may be watching you or — better — filming you.

>> Culturally, it's inappropriate to reach out and shake a woman's hand. Wait for her to offer it. I would apply the same rule to men as well; if they don't extend their hand first, don't reach for it.

>> Grab the hand firmly and release. Let go. If you want, you can grab their elbow with your other hand, which is more intimate.

>> When Ronald Reagan shook hands, he extended his index finger along the other person's wrist. Doing so strengthens your hand muscles and lessens the potential for a heavy handshaker to crush your wrist.

>> Avoid hugs or other personal interaction unless you really know someone. A sideways hug is more acceptable than a full embrace.

>> Practice making eye contact. Ask a friend to help you rehearse how you introduce yourself and keep looking in their eyes. Fortunately, eye contact makes most Americans nervous, so only a few can keep it up for any length of time.

SMALL-TALK TIPS

Good topics for small talk:

- The weather

- Local sports teams

- Family, kids in school

- Vacations

- Any noncontroversial topic in the news

Horrid topics for small talk:

- Recent divorce, legal action, bankruptcy

- Terminal medical conditions

- National politics and religion

- Gossip

- How fat the person has become

Longtime House speaker Tip O'Neill was fond of "pressing the flesh." When he couldn't recall details about someone, he quietly asked, "How's your back?" He asked because most older adults have back issues. The person would be amazed that Tip cared to remember something so personal.

Dressing the part

Hollywood central casting, politician division, has an easy task: Culturally, Americans have a strong mental image of how candidates running for office present themselves. Use that image as your guide. Even if the locals dress casually, remember that you're out for a job interview. People who dress well are taken seriously.

The spectrum of dressing well varies, depending on what's culturally accepted as business dress or business casual for your area. Overdressing would be just as bad as showing up like you're about to mow the lawn. As a general guide, at a candidate forum you must be able to tell the difference between the candidates and members of the general public based on how they dress.

>> Take your cues from others. If possible, look at past elections to see how the winners dressed.

>> Overdressing can be a turnoff. Again, use other candidates and elected officials as a guide. Don't overdress — dress smart.

>> If you find yourself overdressed, take off your jacket and roll up your sleeves.

>> Dressing well is a positive way to boost a weak or unknown reputation.

>> Always wear a campaign name tag in public. Put the tag on your right side, not the left. That way, when you reach out your hand, the other person's eyes naturally follow your arm up to the name tag.

>> Clothing is not a legitimate campaign expense, outside of campaign T-shirts and other giveaways. Wearing a campaign T-shirt to a rally is perfectly fine. See Chapter 11.

To Become a Public Person

Without knowing an elected official, a celebrity, or any European royalty, it's difficult to understand what it truly means to become a public person. Yes, a lot of prestige comes with the job, along with some nice perks. On the other end, higher expectations are required. As you up for the scrutiny?

Being available

The mayor's phone rings at 3:00 in the morning. It's never good news. Placing the phone into Do Not Disturb mode isn't an option, either. Public service demands that you take the 3:00 A.M. call and deal with the consequences. It's an obligation that comes with the job.

Family is a priority, which the public understands. Beyond that, if you win public office, you're beholden to the public — all of them, not just your supporters. This means some of the details about yourself that you might prefer to keep private are now in the public realm.

Elected officials have email addresses at the organization. Some long-term incumbents may be holdouts, but newly minted elected officials are assigned email addresses. These are made available to the public.

During the campaign, you can set up a public email or use your personal email. I've always put one of my personal email accounts on my campaign materials. That's part of the job. If you don't want people emailing you and asking questions, don't run for office.

Your phone number should also be included in your campaign material. If you get elected, your personal phone number will be on the government-issued business card. You can opt for a second cell phone, but I put my primary phone number on both my campaign material and government business card.

» You don't have to answer every phone call. I would recommend answering all local calls just in case, but everything else can go to voicemail. Always return voicemail.

» Respond to any call or email regarding your campaign or public office.

» Studies show that people who respond within 24 hours to an email are thought to be more competent than people who let email linger. An empty inbox is a positive thing.

» You need not respond to all messages. One woman left me a voicemail explaining that she wouldn't vote for me because I had the seat number wrong on my campaign flyer. I didn't respond.

» Keep your appointments. People who meet with you privately expect you to show up. Blowing off a voter or any other citizen is bad form and has consequences.

» Be prompt. Don't be on time — be early. I often show up early so that I can buy my own coffee or tea. Doing so avoids an awkward sense of obligation and keeps me on neutral ground with whoever I'm meeting.

Making new friends and contacts

Running for office allows you to meet people you wouldn't otherwise interact with; cultivate new friendships. If you prefer to be home with a book, don't run for public office.

Never be dismissive of anyone. Friends and confidants may direct you not to meet with someone or to avoid certain people. Shun such advice. You need everyone's support to get the most votes. Just because someone close to you may have an issue with a political activist or other individual doesn't mean you must adopt their posturing.

Always be interested in what people have to say. For the most part, they'll do the talking. If not, when they ask, "Why are you running?" answer them briefly and add a follow-up question: "What would you like to see done?" Engage them. Everyone has a story to tell. People want to be heard.

Cutting short a boring conversation

As a candidate or eventually an elected official, you'll be out in public attending meetings and hobnobbing with supporters and other members of the public. Eventually, someone will approach you and attempt to monopolize your time. This fascinating person could have a compelling story or be a truly noisome pest. Your desire is to flee the conversation.

The simplest way to move on is to tell the other person sincerely, "I don't mean to waste your time." You can also try, "I know you're busy and there are so many other people here." You're referring to yourself, of course, but the other person doesn't hear that, which makes this trick effective: They end the conversation and you're free to move on.

>> While campaigning, it's important that you spend your time wisely and not let a well-intended supporter take it from you. The more time you spend with one person, the less time you have for others.

>> Some devious supporters of your opponent will consume your time deliberately. While you're campaigning door-to-door, they may debate you or otherwise engage you to the point that you'll be unable to meet your door-knocking quota. Be mindful that such people exist.

>> If you have a campaign helper with you, brief them before the event. Offer a signal — for example, putting your right hand on your left shoulder or stepping on your own foot. This clue alerts your assistant to come forward and help you end the conversation. The helper should come over and say your name, adding, "Someone over here would like to speak with you." And you're free.

Chapter 5

Research the Position

L uke was a great candidate. He looked and dressed the part. He was articulate and friendly. At a forum, however, he was asked a question about the position he was running for. The answer was known to anyone who attended a public meeting or even read the paper. Alas, Luke's answer was completely wrong. The voters instantly knew that Luke had failed to do his homework.

Local elected positions require more of a candidate than knowing you'll be on cable channel 98 twice a month. Being a good candidate means you've researched the position, you understand the obligations and know simple facts about the organization, and you've done your homework. These steps provide an important foundation for a successful run for office.

The Obligations of Holding Office

It's surprising how many people don't know that holding elected office is like taking on a part-time job. It's a consistent commitment that can last several years. Time is spent beyond the public meetings. You have homework to do, papers to read, and people to meet. Understand these obligations before you take the initial steps.

Knowing the basic requirements

All public offices have basic requirements, often written in code or statutes. This list includes who is eligible to hold the office, the office term, scheduled responsibilities, salary and benefits, and other items.

For government entities served by an elected board, a staffer is responsible for items like meeting schedules, rules, and other details. This person is often titled the *clerk*. The clerk is your best resource for learning about the basic requirements of the job.

For administrative elected positions, a staffer may be appointed to assist you with the various responsibilities and duties. Organizations and associations related to the position, such as the state board of coroners, might also be of assistance if you have questions about the basic requirements for a position.

The human resources department for the organization might be another resource, though when you're elected, you meet with them eventually anyway.

>> Eligibility for a position depends primarily on whether you're an elector for the district you plan to represent. An *elector* is a qualified resident (not just a property owner) who has lived in the district for a prescribed amount of time and is eligible to vote.

>> Confirm with the local election authority that you're eligible to run for an office before you make further commitments.

>> Special qualifications may include legal or law enforcement experience for certain positions. For example, an elected district attorney must be a lawyer who is licensed to practice law in the jurisdiction.

>> Oddly enough, not every jurisdiction requires that an elected coroner have a medical degree.

>> I suppose elected dogcatchers should be free of dog allergies.

>> Know the term of office! It could be two, three, four, or more years. During this term, you must maintain residency in the district to hold your position.

REMEMBER

>> Ensure that you can make the meeting schedule. The voters will be terribly disappointed if you can't make the regular Thursday Library Board meetings because it's your bowling night.

>> At the bottom of your list should be the position's salary and benefits package. Be aware that some elected positions offer no compensation other than the honor to serve. Other positions offer a monthly stipend, usually enough to cover the cost of gas. For the rest, the benefit package is luxurious, including full medical and retirement, phone fees, use of the cabana at the Bellagio, and similar perks that come with local office.

Exploring other responsibilities

If you've been paying attention to local elected boards, you may notice that some people are chronically absent, yet they keep the job. That's because attendance is based on bare minimums.

For example, your locality may require that an official attend only one meeting every three months to remain qualified for the position. If you're elected, I hope you strive to do better.

Hours required for the job go beyond the posted meeting times. With each meeting comes a packet of material, staff reports, and other data you're expected to become familiar with before the meeting. Do you have the time to study the material?

Review any existing conflicts you have, especially obligations to your children if they still live at home. Family must be a priority, and if you're the key transportation to and from ball practice or ballet lessons, how will that duty affect your public service?

Be aware of unscheduled meetings and workshops. These crop up every so often. An occasional absence due to family or work is okay, but chronic absence is unacceptable to the people you're representing. The good news is that advance notice is required for public meetings. No one in government likes surprises.

REMEMBER

>> Another point to consider is travel. How often are you out of town? Will regular work trips interfere with your public service?

>> If you're elected, remember to inform the clerk or another administrative official of future absences. Don't just skip out on a meeting. Staff must know if you won't attend, to ensure that a quorum is present.

>> Obviously, medical emergencies are excusable.

DAN SAYS

>> A lot of public officials — too many — wing it during meetings. My favorite trick to expose them is to reference a specific item in the packet. I'll say, "On page 49, you see that the figures don't really add up." The way I know few of my peers have looked at the packet comes from the overt page shuffling that follows my statement.

>> The sad part is that an elected official sees no punishment for not studying before a meeting. Only the voters can retire a lazy elected official, and few do.

Fit the Job into Your Schedule

Most people can juggle only three ongoing activities. One of them must be your personal life, which includes your immediate family. Another is your job. If you're elected, the third will be your elected position and then something else must be pushed out. This new top-three item means that anything else that's ongoing in your life must be pushed aside. Are you ready for that?

Between family and work, what regular meetings and appointments do you have? Can you give up any to make room for your public service?

Does your job entail that you must be on call or otherwise available at all hours? If so, you must consider that now might not be the best time for you to hold public office.

REMEMBER

>> You have other ways to get involved. Being an activist or serving on a committee doesn't carry the same responsibility as holding elected office. Further, it's a good way to build your public reputation for a future run, when time is more plentiful and your obligations less severe. Refer to Chapter 3 for other ways to effect change.

>> If you're studying the organization (and you should be), what have you noticed regarding meetings and scheduling? Use your knowledge to see whether serving fits in well with your schedule.

>> One reason you see so many older people hold public office is that they've freed up one of the three ongoing activities in their lives. For example, they're retired or their family hates them.

Study the Issues

Joining an elected body is like catching a moving train: To make a smooth transition, you must get up to speed on the issues. Your knowledge not only helps you tackle issues if elected but also helps during the campaign as it makes you come across as knowledgeable and informed.

To discover what the issues are, attend the meetings. If the agency has a YouTube channel, watch some of the previously recorded meetings. Get a feel for what's important, what the body discusses, and what the public says.

The meeting agenda should be available online. Better still is the meeting *packet*, which is the collection of staff reports and supporting material given to the elected officials. If this document is available online, download and read it. The more you can do this in advance, the better you'll come across as a candidate who under-stands, and has studied, the issues.

If you're a budget hawk (and everyone on the campaign trail claims to be so, despite that not being the case), obtain a copy of the agency's budget. Ensure that it contains data for the past few years so that you can watch spending habits. Con-sider making an appointment with the agency's CFO or treasurer to ask some questions.

To really go the distance, check in on the agency's subcommittees. They should have a public meeting notice and a published agenda and be open to the public. Attend a few or watch them online if they're recorded.

WARNING

>> As you get into the issues, you'll discover that they aren't always clear-cut — right or wrong. Most of the simple issues are covered in the code or rules, which easily address common problems.

>> Knowing about an issue is important, as is being able to explain it to the public. Avoid overly technical explanations in your campaign material and in public forums.

>> The worst thing you can do as a candidate for local office is to inject divisive national political issues into the campaign. Local government provides services and solves limited issues, not anything you see on cable news. Many voters dislike seeing national issues, and the accompanying animosity, injected into a local race.

The Players

At a typical school board meeting, you see the trustees. You may recognize the chairman. Other officials may be known to you as well: the superintendent, finance director, attorney, and so on. Even more staff are present, each with a title and position important enough to attend the meeting. If you expect to join the organization, it helps to know who those people are and what they do.

Recognizing the cast and crew

Before you run, get to know who-does-what in the organization you want to join. Here's a list of public employees based on category of service:

Elected officials: These are the people who already hold office. They act as the executive board of the organization, setting policy, resolving issues not dealt with specifically in the code, and making long-term strategic decisions.

Executive officer: This person serves as the organization's chief administrator. In an educational setting, they're the superintendent or president. They supervise the day-to-day operations of the organization. For single officeholders, this is the position you'll occupy, usually with the assistance of a deputy.

Department heads: These fine people run specific areas of operation within the organization. They might also be called *chiefs, superintendents, directors,* or other fancy titles. These positions are not elected. The people serving as department heads are experts who offer advice but also manage groups of people.

Workers and employees: These are the folks who get the work done, carrying out specific tasks as directed within the organization. You may recognize some of them from meetings. It's good to know their names and understand their positions.

Committee chairs: These are citizen volunteers who run the various committees, generate reports, and carry out specific tasks. Committees have staff associated with them, but they report directly to the elected officials. Chairs are chosen by the committee members, though they could be appointed directly by the board or chief executive, like a mayor or town council chairman.

It's a positive factor for your campaign if you know and recognize the names of these people. Some you'll learn naturally as you attend meetings and read minutes and other documents. When asked, you should be able to recognize, at minimum, a name and the person's function within the organization.

>> To make a business analogy, elected officials are the board of directors. They set policy and make broad decisions. The executive officer carries out the directions of the board, but also follows code that's already established. Other staff carry out specific functions within the organization.

>> The benefit to knowing someone's name in the organization is that it makes you seem knowledgeable and confident. For example, when someone asks a school board candidate about science classes, you can name-drop: "I'll definitely bring that up with Bob Fibonacci, the curriculum director, to see what he thinks."

REMEMBER

>> You may not know their names, but they will definitely know yours! All candidates are known by people within the organization. After all, someday you may be their boss.

Making the rounds

Even if you know the names and positions of the leaders and key members of the organization you plan on joining, make a point to visit with them. Work through the list and ask for an hour of their time.

At the meeting, explain that you're eager to learn what they do. People enjoy talking about their jobs. I find that government employees are excited to share their activities with members of the public. They truly appreciate it when candidates come to visit and show an interest in what they do.

CAMPAIGN CALENDAR

TIP

>> Plan on making your visits well before the campaign begins.

>> It's important that you ask what major issues are approaching, which helps you gain an insider's perspective. Knowing the issues also gives you talking points during the campaign.

>> Don't use your time with a government official to gather dirt on your opponents. Government employees are professionals, and they know to stay out of politics.

>> If the agency is small, you may need to meet only with the administrator or specific chiefs.

>> Some agencies may be so small as to lack any full-time staff. If so, obtain a copy of the meeting minutes to see who shows up to give reports. Make it a point to contact those people.

Identifying other people to know

You might find value in meeting with people outside of the organization. These include community leaders, influential people, and even some of the activists and gadflies. Listen to their perspectives.

Other people who are important to know, though you need not make an appointment with them, include members of the press. Know their names. Know specifically which reporter covers the agency where you seek office.

It's also important to know who runs the election. The agency itself may run the election, or it may be handled by another organization, the county, or even the state directly. Know where the elections office is located and who is the chief elections officer or registrar of voters.

WARNING

» Don't ask for support from community leaders, influential people, activists, or gadflies — not yet. Showing your interest is important. If you sense that someone may support you, contact them later.

» Don't waste the media's time introducing yourself. A simple press release does that for you. The media may conduct candidate interviews during the campaign. Otherwise, don't contact a reporter directly unless you have a story to give them.

» See Chapter 9 for information on building your media contacts list.

Chapter **6**

Consider Your Competition

I f you know what it takes to be a good candidate, you should easily spot potential other candidates for the same position. Call them your potential opposition. These looming opponents may not run for the same office or even the same seat. Some of them are too smart for that. Yet, as part of your campaign strategy, at some early point you must consider your competition and devise a plan to run against that person — or the mob.

Meet Your Opposition

No, you're not the only citizen who desires to hold public office. Others are eager to jump into the fray. Some of them you'll never guess; any fool can run for office, and many of them win. Still, it's possible to examine a list of potential opponents, people who would make good candidates and may rise to oppose you.

Finding possible opponents

Living in Southern California, my family would occasionally make the pilgrimage to Disneyland. During the early morning drive, I'd see all the other cars on the freeway and wonder how many of them were also going to Disneyland. If they all were, the lines would be long and the day miserable.

Similarly, you can look at every valid elector in a political district as a potential opponent in your desire to seek office. That really isn't the case, however. Instead, what you should seek out is who among the potential opponents would make a good candidate.

Before you make a list, study some of the obvious signs that someone is interested in running for office. Consider people who are members of the organization's committees and subcommittees. People who regularly attend meetings may have a high interest in running. Favorite appointees and friends of those in power may also be lured into an election.

Within the community, look for high-profile people in service organizations, who serve on local boards or are active in public events. These are the type of people who frequently get elected, because they're a known quantity and they show a dedication to, and interest in, serving the public.

Don't rule out any activists or gadflies. People with a single issue are often driven into a race. They may not be good candidates, but they could be potential opponents.

If the list of possible contenders grows long, take heart. Just like cars on the freeway going to Disneyland, not everyone you guess as a possible opponent will step up and run.

Building a list of potential candidates

After surveying the political landscape and scouting out potential opponents, work on creating a list. Consider this process to be early opposition research. It may also have the blessing of you finding someone you'd rather support as opposed to running yourself. Otherwise, look at the list and remind yourself out loud, "How dare any of these people run against me!"

Study each opponent for potential strengths and weaknesses. See the later section "Doing a SWOT analysis" for assistance. You're not performing this step to tear anyone down, but rather to size up the competition, should someone on your list choose to run.

Another way to look at the list is to consider that your desire isn't to run. Instead, you're looking for a good candidate to represent yourself. Who rises to the top? Who can be easily dismissed?

As an exercise, add yourself to the list. Where do you fit in? Who on the list is a better candidate, and who is worse?

Doing a SWOT analysis

A good tool for reviewing potential opposition is the SWOT analysis. SWOT is an acronym representing the four corners of a matrix: Strengths, Weaknesses, Opportunities, and Threats. Running a SWOT analysis can help you size up opponents and also examine your own position as a competitive candidate.

Figure 6-1 shows an empty SWOT matrix. It serves as an exercise to help you achieve certain goals. To work it, you must fill in the grid: Internal helpful items are strengths; internal harmful items are weaknesses; external helpful items are opportunities; and external harmful items are treats.

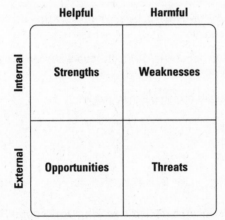

FIGURE 6-1:
The SWOT matrix.

Everyone running for office has weaknesses and strengths. Use your list of potential opponents to examine each one in their own SWOT chart. As candidates announce, you can perform a more detailed analysis, which will help you craft your campaign.

TIP

Before you start guessing about potential opponents, fill in your own SWOT chart. Be honest! Draw up each of the squares. Figure 6-2 shows an example.

	Helpful	**Harmful**
Internal	• Outstandingly handsome • Married for 14 years • Regularly attend church • Chess club president	• Had plastic surgery • Wife hates me • Known alcoholic • Stole money from the club
External	• Low-profile race • Public record expunged • People owe me money • Guido said he'd help	• Reporter snooping around • Ex-business partner out on bail • Guido says I'll owe him a favor

FIGURE 6-2:
A sample SWOT matrix, filled in.

When you have your SWOT chart filled in, you can work to address noted weaknesses and threats and build upon your strengths and opportunities.

>> Everyone running for office has a weakness. You do, too.

>> Incumbents specifically have weaknesses. Whom have they ticked off? Which votes caused public outcry?

>> One item to put in your opponents' Strength square is where they may garner their support.

>> See Chapter 12 for details on campaign strategies.

The Street Fight

A seat is open, and the incumbent isn't seeking reelection. This opportunity unlocks the floodgates for anyone wanting to seek office. It's far easier to take an unoccupied seat than it is to wrestle one from an established incumbent.

Having too many opponents

The American political system is *binary*, which is traditional but also favored by the parties and the media, who enjoy framing all politics in terms of a bad guy and a worse guy. The ideal race for office is two people. You'll be lucky if you see that few for an open seat.

The advantage of having too many opponents is that you need to capture fewer votes to win. In a 5-way race, the winner may receive only 25 percent of the total votes. True, that means that 75 percent of the voters preferred someone else, but that's how our system works.

Odds are better, however, that multiple people in a race means only two or three will be taken as serious candidates. It's easy for the electorate to quickly dismiss someone who's running on a lark or who has a single issue. Some people run for office so that they can grandstand and speak in public. The problem they present is that you and your message get lost in the noise.

If it's your fate to be in a street fight, run a positive campaign showcasing your talents. Be aware of and single out serious opposition. Ignore the rest.

Categorizing your opposition

I've never seen a race for office with more than three people seeking the same seat where there isn't an obvious fool in the mix. After the filing deadline and before the race begins, categorize your opponents. The best way to do so is to phone them up and chat.

You need not phone the serious candidates, those you've already placed on your list. (Refer to the earlier section "Building a list of potential candidates.") Phone up the rest. Introduce yourself. Ask them why they're seeking office. They'll be happy to talk, enjoying the attention. You'll quickly be able to size them up and determine who is in the race just for fun.

The nonserious candidates don't deserve your attention. Otherwise, somewhere in the mix you'll find some big dogs. Do a SWOT chart on them, and ask your friends and political allies what they think of the race now that you have true opposition. The race is still winnable, but you must work hard.

DAN SAYS

>> Refer to the earlier section "Doing a SWOT analysis" for details on the SWOT chart.

>> Your phone call to the nonserious candidates will most likely be the only political phone call they receive during the campaign.

>> I refer to people who run for office on a lark as the *5 percenters*. These people generally get less than 5 percent of the vote when more than three people are running for the same office.

Dropping out

When you find yourself in a street fight, where more than three people are seeking the same office, look closely at your chief competitors. If one of them supports your same platform to a certain degree, consider dropping out of the race and endorsing them. Then go to work for their campaign.

The problem with staying in a race where two people support the same ideas is that you're diluting your base. You're two apples along with an orange, a melon, and a pear; people see only "apple" as a choice and not individual candidates.

The advantage of dropping out is that your goal in office will hopefully still be met by the other candidate. Further, you earn major kudos from others in the political arena who will remember what you did.

If dropping out isn't to your liking, or specifically your ego, get the other guy to drop out. Hold a meeting and discuss your similarities but also showcase your personal strengths. In fact, while you're at it, try to convince some of the nonserious candidates to drop out of the race as well. Ask them. Tell them that you've been studying the issues and are willing to spend your own money to win. You may not convince them to drop from the race, but who knows?

The Formidable Foe (an Incumbent)

If it's your desire to get into a 2-way race, you most definitely want to run against an incumbent. Most potential candidates wait for an open seat, one vacated by an incumbent. When the current officeholder seeks reelection, however, most candidates steer clear of the race. The odds just aren't in your favor.

>> The *incumbent* is the current officeholder who is seeking reelection.

>> An incumbent's most vulnerable election is their second, which is the first time they run for *reelection*. After that, incumbents become entrenched and are extremely difficult to unseat.

>> Another weakness is when an incumbent is a midterm replacement. They've never run for the seat; therefore, their reelection is really their first election.

Studying the incumbent's record

The good news about running against an incumbent is that they have a public record. They could prattle on about how they'll fight to keep taxes low during the election, but does their voting record in office reflect that promise?

Look at two factors if it's your desire to take on an incumbent: their term in office and their bad decisions.

Americans may bemoan how people in Congress have been around for 30 years and how it's part of the problem, but locally Americans seem to be okay with eternal officeholders. If the incumbent is popular and wins reelection handily every time, consider another seat.

On the other hand, longevity in office leads to a certain comfort level with the status quo. Play up on that if you plan on running. Also note how the incumbent may be fading, not as willing to fight as before. This tactic can backfire, so approach it by thanking them for their service and urging them to step down and let a new generation with new energy take on the role.

Easier than longevity is capitalizing on the incumbent's voting record — specifically, unpopular decisions. Remember, *they* must defend their record. You merely take the other side. Alas, even with a series of missteps and gaffes, it remains a tall order to unseat an incumbent.

Reviewing the organization's unpopular decisions

Even if your incumbent opponent has a good record, consider using the entire organization's record in your campaign. How well is the organization run? How often does public opinion go against the positions taken by the organization? And what is your opponent's record in standing up for the public when the organization makes a bad move?

Your success with this approach depends on facts. You cannot create an issue that isn't there. And even if the issue exists, you gain no traction if the public isn't aware of it before you campaign.

Experiencing the perfect political storm

Incumbents are unseated by a perfect political storm of opportunity. The pieces include bad decisions, a general dislike, motivated voters, and good name recognition for the challenger.

The bad decisions must be public and publicly disliked. All elected officials make bad decisions. What you seek is an incumbent who chronically makes bad decisions. Better still is when they stubbornly defend the decisions in the face of an outraged public.

Even when you find the perfect storm, it may still take two election cycles to purge the incumbent. Especially in partisan races, as long as the incumbent survives the primary, if the district's color matches that of the incumbent's jersey, they win — no matter how odious their behavior.

The Agony of Running Unopposed

It would be wonderful if everyone recognized your brilliance and decided to step aside and let you run unopposed for the seat you desire. Unless you find an opportunity to run for an open seat that no one else wants, or you're an incredibly popular incumbent, running unopposed isn't in the cards.

>> If it's your desire to take a first-time run unopposed, look for a low-interest, low-turnout election. This process takes some effort. Refer to Chapter 2 for information on finding political divisions in which you reside that are well off the radar.

>> The drawback to finding an office no one else wants is that the exposure will be low by default. If it's your desire to climb the political ladder, you must start on a higher rung.

DAN SAYS

>> I've run unopposed as an incumbent (though, technically, my last-minute opponent dropped from the race before the deadline). I found it disappointing, because I never got the chance to defend my record and I was left out of the debates and forums. These activities are part of the political process, and it seems awkward to be left out.

Slates

Some people find strength in running with others, two candidates for separate seats on the same board. The advantage is that you can run together and play off each other's strengths. The disadvantage is that when one candidate makes a horrid blunder, both share the retribution.

Understanding a slate

Slating is a way for candidates in nonpartisan races to build group momentum. As in a partisan race, the slate can claim, "We all believe in these things and will accomplish them in office." Because the public has been trained by the two big parties and media to view politics in a binary fashion, slating is natural to the voter.

The advantage of slating is that you share your message with others. You naturally have another champion out campaigning for you, recommending you to a group of people you don't know.

The disadvantage of slating is that your group is only as strong as its weakest member. Before aligning yourself publicly with other candidates, ensure that you're okay with whatever baggage they bring into your election.

Just as the admiration of a single candidate in the slate can rally people to vote for you, disgust with one candidate in a slate can rally people not to vote for you. Slating is a touchy topic.

>> Slating isn't necessary for a partisan office, in that the party automatically creates the slate for you.

>> If you chose not to slate, avoid answering the question of which other candidates in the race you support. Say, "I'm focusing on my own race." Anything else you say will spread like fire through dry kindling and not do you any good.

>> Privately, it's okay to support and encourage other candidates, such as people you already work with or want to work with in office. Still, the truth is that whoever gets elected must work with you, should you win.

>> Don't slate. It's okay to admire other candidates, but run your own campaign.

DAN SAYS

Being slated against your will

Bill and Sue decide to run for the two open school board seats. As former PTO parents, they form a slate and run as a team. You're running for the same seat as Bill. A strong critic of the school board, disliked by most people in town, is running against Sue. Because Bill and Sue are slated, you and the critic are slated as well.

The public enjoys team sports, and if you're unfortunate enough to be a single candidate running against a member of a slate, you will be slated. More common is when each incumbent has a single opponent. Then the slate becomes the insiders-versus-the-challengers. The road gets rough because any doofus challenge drags down the entire group — even though you're not a slate.

The best way to deal with being slated against your will is to focus on your own campaign. When asked why another challenger said something stupid, reply that you're running your own campaign against Mr. Incumbent and you think the voters want him out — or whatever. Keep the focus on your individual race.

Conversely, you can also use the most disliked member of a slate against your opponent if he or she is a member of that slate. Go for the red meat if a single member of the slate messes up during the campaign. Pointedly ask the person what they think about the other candidate's mistake. Give 'em hell.

Chapter **7**

Know the Voters

Voters are fickle yet necessary people, often wrong and fabulously underinformed. Our system of government relies upon voters to thrust candidates into office, worthy or not. It's your job as a candidate to convince enough of them that you can better represent their interests than your opponents. It's these voters — impulsive, given unto emotion, and illogical — who make politics more of an art than a science.

Behold: Voter Data!

Your personal voting record is held in confidence; whom you voted for is private, and you mark your ballot anonymously. The fact that you voted, however, is a public record. Further, information about your voter registration is available to anyone who asks. Cumulatively, your voting record, and that of every voter in the district, is valuable data to any candidate.

» The voting booth is private, but data regarding whether you voted and your voter registration are public.

» *Voter data* includes your party affiliation, address, and any other details you've offered when you registered to vote, such as your phone number or email.

>> The reason for keeping voter data is to ensure that people are valid electors in their districts. For example, only city residents can vote in a city election. Your voter registration shows your full-time residence, which is what determines in which districts you can vote.

Running the local election

To gather voter data, you must know which government agency handles elections for the office you seek. In many cases, a county agency conducts elections and manages the voter data, even for local elections. For rural locations and smaller districts, it may be the government entity itself that handles the election.

Before you begin your campaign, seek out the agency that holds voter data. You need this data for your mailing lists, walking lists, phone lists, and so on. See the next section.

>> Throughout this book, the agency that runs the local election is referred to as the election authority.

>> In most states, the chief elections officer is the secretary of state. This office oversees all voters and elections, though local entities may run the elections.

>> At the local level, a county officer may oversee all elections. The title varies: supervisor of elections, registrar of voters, county clerk.

>> The entity that runs local elections might also be the entity with which you register to become a candidate. See Chapter 8.

TIP

>> If you're completely in the dark as to who runs the election, phone up the government entity where you seek office and ask them.

Gathering election data

Before you begin your campaign, obtain some voter lists. These are public records, and most election authorities offer the data to anyone who asks. You may be required to fill in a request form, which is fine. A fee may be associated with the request.

Have the request filled electronically; you do not want a paper copy. The voter list may be available in plain text format, Excel, or some type of database. I recommend getting the list in Excel format. Most direct mail marketing firms use Excel when they send bulk mail.

The agency managing the voter registration lists doesn't filter the voter data for you. Some agencies may allow you to specifically request voter data within a specific district. If so, request that your list include only currently registered voters for the political division where you seek office: the city, school district, fire district, and so on. Otherwise, obtain the entire list, which you must filter. (See the next section.)

Request to receive historical voter data. You want to gather voting records that go back at least four years. Lists that go back longer are better, but you risk including that voters have moved. The historical voter data helps you build a list of frequent voters, people who vote in all elections — even the small elections. These people are your key demographic.

Ensure that the voter data lists physical and mailing addresses. The physical address is what determines in which elections a voter is qualified. The mailing address is where voters receive mail. You want to send your material only to the mailing address.

Other details are helpful in the list, including party registration, phone numbers, and email. The more data, the better.

Beyond the voter list, also request election results and turnout data for prior elections. These items can help you determine your campaign strategy and budget.

Turnout details help you gauge how big of a campaign you must run. If an average of 2,400 people vote in your library district, count on that number of voters to turn out for your election. Use this rule as a guide because many factors determine voter turnout.

Also review how current officeholders fared in past elections. If you're running against an incumbent, see whether the past few elections have showed a downward trend. If so, the officeholder's enchantment with the public may be waning.

REMEMBER

>> The election authority may prohibit members of the public from using voter data for advertising or solicitation purposes. For running a political campaign, however, the voter roll is fair game.

>> The fee you pay for voter data is a campaign expense. Remember to record it as such. Not every elections office charges for the data.

>> Be aware that voter lists become obsolete quickly. Even the most current list has invalid data in it. I don't use lists from prior elections.

>> You need voter data only for the district in which you're running. Do not obtain the full voter list unless the elections office is unable to provide a specific list. (If so, removing unqualified voters becomes *your* job.)

>> See Chapter 12 for information how to use the voter lists.

Preparing your lists

The purpose of gathering historical voter data is to identify and target key voters in your election. You use the information for mailing and phoning and when going door-to-door. Yard signs and billboards aren't as effective as targeting specific, frequent voters.

To make the most of the voter data, you must prepare specific lists. This task requires a bit of skill in Excel, assuming that it's the file format for the voter data. If you're not adept at using Excel, find a campaign volunteer to assist you. Good lists are valuable to your campaign, so paying someone to massage them is a worthy expense.

You'll likely create multiple specific lists from the master voter list that's provided. Make copies of that file so that each list is held in its own file.

I recommend creating these lists:

>> Chronic voters

>> A walking list

>> Targeted mailing lists

>> An absentee list

The following sections go over specifics for each list.

The chronic-voter list

The voter database contains a lot of people who have moved, who don't vote, or who vote only in presidential elections. Somewhere in that list, however, you'll find *chronic voters* — these are your key demographic, the people who vote in every single election.

To create the list, look at the voter's history. You want on the list only people who have voted in every election held over the past few years. In Excel, you can sort the list by the previous elections' columns to see which rows offer these valued voters.

Chronic voters are important because they don't miss elections. They *will* vote in your election. If your campaign can afford it, you must send material to every chronic voter. It's far easier to persuade a chronic voter to vote for you than it is to persuade a casual voter.

A walking list

Going door-to-door is a time-honored campaign tradition. The goal is to knock on voters' doors and not waste time with people who don't vote. Your voter list helps you make this determination.

A good walking list is about logistics. Like the post office delivering mail, you want a list that most efficiently covers an area. Use your chronic-voter list as a base because it contains people certain to vote in your election. Divide the list into the smallest political division, such as a precinct.

Within each list, organize the voters by street and then in order by house number. For most locations, this level of organization is good enough, though if you have volunteers who know the area, divide the list by neighborhood. Such a task can't really be done automatically, but it saves time to do so in advance rather than shuffle papers while you walk.

See Chapter 12 for more information on campaigning door-to-door.

Specific lists for targeted mailers

If your campaign budget is huge, you can send out multiple mailers to everyone on your chronic-voters list. I know of no one who has a huge campaign budget, so the third type of voter list you want must be highly focused. It's a subset of the chronic voter.

For example, create a list that shows only voters who vote in your specific election. These people may skip other elections, yet they show a focus on the district where you desire a seat. Call them chronic district voters.

Peruse prior years' election data to see in which precincts or areas an incumbent opponent has done poorly. Create lists that target those areas, and create specific mailers that focus on those voters.

Determine which elections have lower turnout. Create a list of people who voted in those elections, especially when incumbents ran unopposed. These are your die-hard voters, and you want to reach out to them.

Creating a targeted mailer list may seem like more work, but the effort pays off. The cost of direct mail to these voters is worthy.

A list of absentee voters

Another list you need is one showing those people who show a preference for voting absentee. This list is specific to those locations where absentee voting is held. States where all elections are by mail work differently.

Peruse the collected election data to cull those voters who vote absentee. Create a list, a subset of the chronic-voters list, that shows only those voters. The goal is to hit them up early. You want to send out a heads-up because all of them vote well before the general election.

Also see the later section, "Obtaining ongoing voter data." This step is the second approach in reaching early voters, along with the absentee-voter list.

>> Your campaign for office is a marketing campaign. You want to reach your best customers, those people who vote frequently.

>> If you're in a partisan race, you must create lists for two elections — that is, unless your area is so partisan that winning the primary guarantees victory in the general election.

>> Don't mess too much with the list's raw data if you plan to use a direct-mailing firm. Excel can do weird things to large spreadsheets. These changes can upset the special software used by the bulk-mailing houses. Leaving the voter list as unmolested as possible is a good thing.

>> Some campaign managers may insist that you visit every house when door-knocking. They recommend carrying voter registration cards so that you can sign up nonvoters. You can whip up interest for low-frequency voters as well. If you have time, pursue this strategy, though I recommend that you confer with others who've run campaigns in your area, to see whether this approach is an effective use of time.

>> Parties often have lists, so if you're a party member, you might be able to obtain their lists and appeal to voters who share common interests.

Purging the lists

In addition to creating specific voter lists, you must do some eliminating. This step takes place after you've created your chronic voter list, walking list, absentee list, and so. The goal is to remove and combine.

First, you want to remove from the list people you are certain will not vote for you. For example, your opponent. You can also pull out your opponent's supporters and others you're certain aren't casting a vote for you. Eliminating such people from your voter list may seem petty, but this process saves campaign resources.

Second, you must combine multiple voters at the same residence. If five people are registered to vote at 555 Fifth St., you're wasting four stamps and four postcards sending mail to each of them. Instead, create a single record.

For example, if multiple voters at the same residence share their last name, create a single entry: Quintus Household. Bulk mailing services do so automatically.

Another tactic to use is overlaying multiple address labels so that each name appears but only one address. Figure 7-1 illustrates how this technique works.

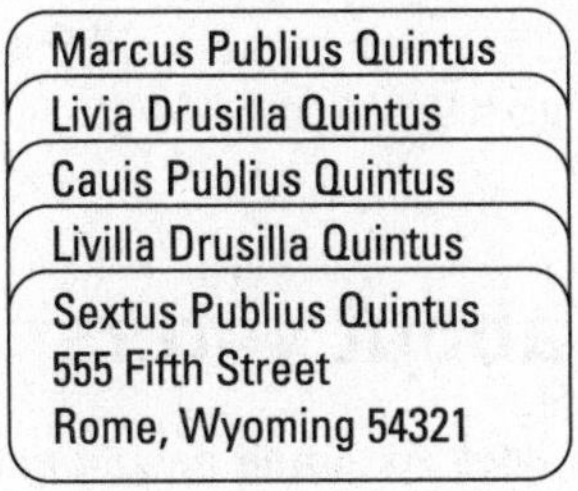

FIGURE 7-1:
Contacting
multiple voters.

```
Marcus Publius Quintus
Livia Drusilla Quintus
Cauis Publius Quintus
Livilla Drusilla Quintus
Sextus Publius Quintus
555 Fifth Street
Rome, Wyoming 54321
```

Obtaining ongoing voter data

The election authority generates voter data as the election unfolds. This new information might also be available to the public. It includes

>> People who have applied for an absentee or vote-by-mail ballot

>> People who have already voted

>> New-voter registrations

If possible, sign up to receive this information as it becomes known. Hopefully, your area's elections office provides the details with little fuss and no fees. If fees are charged, they're worth it. Use this data to contact new voters and to purge from your list the people who've already voted.

See Chapter 12 for more details on using ongoing voter data.

The Fickle Electorate

Americans love elections with a huge turnout. Candidates gush over such elections, too. The feeling is that the turnout justifies the results, just as higher numbers in a survey show a lower margin of error. Huge turnout is great, but only when the electorate is making an informed decision. Lamentably, that happens far less often than you think.

>> Multiple factors affect voter turnout. Presidential elections have the highest turnout and the most interest. Local elections, especially those held outside of the traditional November date, have lower turnout.

>> Hot-topic issues may not affect turnout but do affect who wins. You may think that a poor decision by the organization, one that upsets everyone you know, will cause multitudes to vote. Often it doesn't.

>> I've heard that low-turnout elections favor the incumbents, but also that low-turnout elections favor challengers. Who knows?

DAN SAYS

Accepting the truth about voters

Not everyone who is eligible to vote does so. Some people never register. Even people who register don't vote or vote only in specific elections.

The number of registered voters is probably high in your area, but not 100 percent of all adults who can vote. Further, for each election, only a percentage of registered voters cast ballots. This value is expressed as the *turnout*.

Of all the voters, only a few study the issues. They follow the candidates and make informed decisions. This is good news! Most voters, however, make up their minds close to election day. I've heard that 15 percent of the voters wait until election week to start studying the issues. Ten percent wait until election day. Five percent make up their minds in the voting booth. These figures are generous.

It's disturbing that so many close elections are decided by people who make their choice in the voting booth. These low-information voters can have more effect than those who know the candidates and have studied the issues.

Don't be put off. Your campaign's goal is to make an impression with a majority of those who vote. Remember: You need only 50 percent plus 1 to win, or a plurality of the votes in a multiway race.

>> The *turnout* is defined as the number of people who vote divided by the total number of registered voters in the voting district.

>> You want the people you connect with during the campaign to be so impressed that they inform their friends and neighbors how to vote. This phenomenon, known as *word-of-mouth,* is the best support your campaign can get.

>> A recent off-year election in my county had a record 85 percent turnout. A few years earlier, a school district election had a 4 percent turnout. Regardless of the percentages, people win office and serve the entire public.

DAN SAYS

Dealing with unholy partisanship

Some local elections are partisan, usually for larger districts. In this situation, the lines are drawn and you must declare one side or the other and then hope that your party affiliation helps propel you into office.

In most parts of the country, local offices are nonpartisan. Decisions made by smaller political districts are routine, well off the radar of the major news networks. Still, even with the absence of divisive partisan issues, partisan politics can wend its way in a nonpartisan election.

Thanks to years of training — and to the nonsensical phrase "don't throw away your vote" being ingrained into the American voter's psyche — many people will ask your party preference even in a nonpartisan race. Don't bother arguing with them or explaining that the office has nothing to do with partisan issues. Just fess up and tell them how you're registered. It's disappointing, I know, but forces beyond your control compel people to ask.

DAN SAYS

» Being from one party or another helps the voter know how you align politically. This unholy fact strains the issues because not everyone registered in one party or the other agrees 100 percent with the party platforms. Even at the party conventions, few if any issues pass unanimously.

» If your area leans predominantly one way or the other, associate with that party. Yes, making this move is politically expedient. Still, in every election you'll find candidates who desire to run as independents but must salute one flag or another because that's the sad way our system works.

» Once while door-knocking, I spoke with a voter and noticed in the background Fox News on his TV. When he asked my party affiliation, I said, "I'm a Republican." That was all he needed to hear. He replied, "You have my vote" as he took my literature and closed the door.

Becoming the preferred type of elected official

I've yet to find any citizen who proclaims joyously that every elected official representing them is the best possible person for the job. Even the most partisan extremist will confess, in the deep dark where no one can hear, that they're massively disappointed with some of their own party's elected officials.

The preferred type of elected official, the one everyone loves without question, doesn't exist. Not everyone will agree with you all the time. Though the election is really a popularity contest, winning doesn't ensure long-term popularity.

Take a moment to survey the crop of locally elected officials in your area. These are the people a majority of the voters placed in office. I doubt you'll find in the group more than one or two who meet with unanimous acclaim. If you win your election, you join the lot.

I'm not implying that you're going to be "one of them" — merely that if you win, you soon join their ranks. Brace yourself for such a reality.

**DAN
SAYS**

>> Most elections are about the lesser of two evils. Many people vote *against,* as opposed to voting *for,* a candidate.

>> *Clothespin* voting is the name given to people who vote for someone they don't like to get rid of another candidate they like less.

>> As I often advise potential candidates, everyone wants to be Tom Hanks. Alas, you're not running for Tom Hanks — you're running for public office. You will never be 100 percent popular. Even if you achieve 90 percent popularity, it will be fleeting.

Chapter **8**

Ready to Run

" **Y**ou know, Peaches, I read in the morning paper that it's now filing season for city council. I've a notion to toss my hat into the ring. What say you?"

There's a word for people who decide to join an election at the last minute. That word isn't *victor.* So many tasks must be completed before you take the plunge, not as a legal requirement but rather to set the groundwork for what you hope will be a successful campaign for public office.

When to Start?

Being ready to run means you've chosen an office and, hopefully, know enough about it that you won't appear as one of those candidates who runs just because they seek attention. After laying the groundwork (covered earlier in this book), you may still wonder what exactly comes next. When do you start to run, and how do you know what to do in the proper order?

> » Running for office the first time is like playing a new card game: You can try to read the rules yourself, but it's best to know someone who's already played and have them advise you along the way.

>> You can't really screw anything up if you adhere to the deadlines required by law. See the later section "Creating a campaign calendar." Of course, you want to run a better campaign than something thrown together at the last moment.

Knowing the election type and style

Elections can be classified by type and style. Knowing these details helps you craft a specific campaign. Your goal is to put in only the effort you need to win while not spending too much money.

These are the three broad types of local elections:

>> **General election:** The general election is the only election for the office. You suffer through the election, typically in November, and the winner takes the seat. Easy-peasy.

>> **Primary, general:** For partisan local offices, first comes a primary election, typically in the spring. This election is by party. If you run as a plutocrat, you appear on the plutocratic ballot to win as the representative in the general election in the fall.

>> **Runoff election:** A runoff election typically takes place when no single candidate garners more than 50 percent of the vote. It's a quick turnaround for a second election between the top two vote-getters. The issue here is that you never know when the runoff election takes place or whether you'll be involved.

The election you want is the general election. It's a single event involving one solid campaign.

For the partisan primary and open general election, your hope is that the party kicks in some funds and marketing for the general election. Therefore, your major focus is on the primary.

Runoff elections are frustrating, but only when more than two people are vying for the same office. When you get a street fight, odds are good you'll have a runoff. Plan for that.

The style of election has its options as well:

>> **By seat:** In this election, the officials occupy numbered seats. When you choose to run, you must select a specific seat — say, Seat 3 — and list it on

your candidate application. Other candidates also choose a seat. An incumbent who roosts his haunches in the seat is your opponent.

>> **By district:** You run for a specific seat that represents the area where you live. Only people who live in the area qualify as candidates. Everyone in the district may get to vote for all candidates, or voting may be limited to only the voters in the district.

>> **Horse race:** In this rare type of election, all candidates appear on a single ballot, name only. The top vote-getters (depending on seats available) take office.

Seats are used for at-large representation. You choose a specific seat, but you represent everyone in the district. Likewise, everyone in the district votes for all the seats up for election.

By-district voting ensures that all regions of a larger area are represented. Sometimes a large district may cover rural areas where people feel left out. By creating districts, those people are guaranteed representation.

The horse race is an interesting creature, where the campaign isn't against a specific opponent, as you have in by-seat or by-district races. This type of election allows people to vote for the candidates they like as opposed to voting against someone.

>> Not every local office holds elections in November.

>> In nearly every case, a runoff election is won by the candidate with the majority of the votes in the general election.

>> For by-seat elections, only specific seats are up for election in each cycle. The number depends on the total number of elected officials and the term of office.

>> In some by-district races, an option is available to run for an at-large seat. Any resident of the political subdivision is eligible to run for an at-large seat.

>> If you run by district, find out whether only people in the district can vote for you or the voting is for the entire area. The difference tells you how large of a campaign you need to run.

Creating a campaign calendar

CAMPAIGN CALENDAR

Whether you use Outlook, Google Calendar, or iCal, you benefit from creating a calendar for your campaign. Do it now.

As the campaign gets underway, the calendar fills with various events, forums, meet-and-greets, and so on. Your job is to pack the campaign calendar with looming dates and deadlines regarding the election.

You must adhere to these dates and deadlines as established by election code for the district in which you're running. These deadlines include

>> When to declare as a candidate, first day through last day

>> When to declare a treasurer or campaign committee

>> When you can start raising money

>> When to withdraw from the race

>> When you can put out yard signs

>> When you must file campaign finance reports

>> When early voting, mail-in voting, or absentee voting starts

>> The election day

>> Other deadlines

These dates are written in code, but don't look there! Instead, contact the agency where you seek office. The clerk or another person in charge of the election should have available candidate packets that list all deadlines and other requirements. When you know the details, jot them down in your calendar.

TIP

>> If you're planning ahead, the next election's packet might not be available. If so, check the agency's website for some older packets to get an idea of what's coming up.

>> Refer to Chapter 7 for information on discovering who runs the election.

Starting early

A topic of debate among campaign professionals is when to start running for office. Presidential races once had candidates declaring only a month before the New Hampshire primary. Recently, candidates declare for the presidential race a year or more before the first primary. For your race, where the need to raise billions of dollars is low, the date need not be so distant.

For gearing up your campaign, starting early is important. I would recommend that you study the issues and know the players at least a year before you decide to run. If you wait until the filing period, you have more catching up to do, which means less time to campaign.

The key to determining when to start is the filing period. The goal for most candidates is to ensure that their presence on the ballot will dissuade casual candidates from getting into the race. In your head, you imagine them saying, "No way I'm getting into a race against [*your name here*]!"

I would offer that you announce before the filing period. To be safe, announce *the week before* filing opens. This approach works best if you're the first to announce for a seat, even if it's occupied by an incumbent who has yet to declare. Your action sets up the race.

Another strategy is to wait until the end of the filing period. That way, you can see who else is in the race. If a powerful opponent steps up, you may want to rethink your approach. If the incumbent is running unopposed, that makes you the alternative. And if it's a street fight with a lot of nobodies, perhaps your entering the race forces some of them to drop out.

>> The problem with declaring too early for a local election is that you make waves that disappear by the time the election rolls around. Candidates who announce are given a notice in the local paper, which is worth more when you make the announcement closer to the filing period.

>> If you're curious whether an incumbent will seek reelection, ask them. If not directly, have a friend phone up the officeholder. Incumbents may not formally announce until later, but they often share their desire to run again well before the deadline.

REMEMBER

>> Don't let your opponent's early announcement prompt you to announce as well. In fact, if an opponent announces early, announce late. Spread out the time long enough so that they won't be well prepared for you as competition. And remember that this trick works both ways.

The Announcement

The political gossips already know that you're seeking office. This is good news! If no one knows who you are yet or cares that you're interested in running, you have a major battle ahead of you with regard to name recognition. Regardless, at some point, you must make a formal announcement that you're seeking public office.

Ensure that you have a campaign presence before you announce. You need not have all your material ready, but you must have a website, a few social media sites, a phone number, and an email address. Work these items into your campaign calendar.

>> Making an announcement isn't a must, but it's a positive thing because of the free press.

>> On your campaign calendar, the announcement comes before you file. If you file first, political junkies and astute opponents will know about it and can take the wind from your sails.

Creating a press release

I strongly recommend that you craft a press release for your announcement. Even if you plan to stage an event (see the next section), couple it with a press release. It's your first, best, and least expensive campaign move.

Chapter 12 offers details and suggestions for writing press releases. For your announcement, you must cover these items:

>> **Who you are and which office you seek:** Start your press release with this paragraph. You may also use a hook, such as "I'm tired of parents being ignored by our school board" or the trusty old "Our taxes are too high." The more obvious and well-known the issue, the better.

>> **Why you've decided to run:** List your campaign talking points and key issues. Be positive. Reflect how your experience helps you meet these goals.

>> **Nasty things:** Take a paragraph to briefly sum up things that are going wrong at the agency. Criticize the incumbent's record. Avoid mentioning non-incumbent opponents, because you don't want to draw free press to them.

>> **End positive:** Mention good things you hope to accomplish. Direct voters to your campaign website and social media, and provide other details.

Proofread and double-proofread your press release. It should be one page long at the most, double-spaced. It's not necessary to print the press release on campaign letterhead, but if you have the letterhead, use it. The press release can also be sent out electronically.

Understand that news agencies can print the announcement immediately and may even post it online upon receipt. Don't bother with any "hold for release" notices. Send out your announcement press release only when you're ready to see it published.

- » A press release is free campaign material.

- » Not every media outlet will publish your press release. Don't become emotionally affected by this decision.

- » The press may not print your release for a few days, which shouldn't be interpreted as anything negative.

- » TV news rarely covers local election announcements.

- » Your campaign announcement is probably the only free press you'll receive. Avoid trying to force reporters into being part of your campaign. Even if a reporter privately admits they support you (and that's rare), don't expect any favors — especially if you misstep.

- » See Chapter 9 for details on creating a media list.

- » Chapter 16 offers tips on how to work with the press.

Staging an announcement event

Setting up an announcement event works best in the movies, where extras are paid to wear silly hats, wave banners, cheer on cue, and dish up a healthy slice of Americana. In the real world, an announcement event is dicey.

If you must stage an announcement event, ensure that a significant crowd shows up. Inform the press that you plan on a big crowd and they might attend as well. Take plenty of photos for your campaign material. Live-stream the announcement to social media, and record it later for your website or YouTube.

If you can't guarantee a crowd, don't do an announcement event. It's not necessary to ensure your victory. In fact, if you stage an event and a paltry crowd appears, your opponent may spy on you and use the small number of supporters against you. I would.

- » *You* are responsible for the crowd. The general public won't spontaneously show up. Use your volunteers as your crowd. See Chapter 9 for details on drafting volunteers.

- » Have your campaign material ready at the announcement. Mark your campaign calendar so that you're certain the material is available.

- » For smaller crowds, line up people behind you or in a tight group so that it appears as if more people showed up. This arrangement isn't cheating; national politicians do it all the time.

CAMPAIGN
CALENDAR

TIP

> The press will show up if you tell them a sizable crowd will be there. It's very important that you back your word. If you entice a reporter to attend and you have only a handful of people, you lose credibility. It's tough to earn it back.

> Even with a guaranteed crowd, the press may not show up if you lack a reputation with them.

WARNING

> Avoid making your announcement at a meeting of the government body. Doing so is in poor taste, and it makes the staff uncomfortable. Incumbents don't announce at a meeting. You shouldn't, either.

Get Your Answers Ready

Preparing a run for office requires more than printing banners and waving yard signs. You must also know why you're running for office and have quick answers ready. These answers are part of your homework. They show the voters that you're a serious contender.

> Your answers are for the press, but also any concerned citizens. You provide the answers at forums, go door-to-door, or meet anyone in public during the campaign.

> Showcase your positive attributes first when answering a question.

> Avoid mentioning your opponent unless asked. If asked, do not beat up your opponent, slander them, bad mouth them. Instead, turn the focus back to you and your campaign.

DAN
SAYS

> On the cusp of entering the 1980 presidential election, CBS News reporter Roger Mudd asked Senator Ted Kennedy the now famous and seemingly innocent question, "Why do you want to be President?" Kennedy's awkward pause and subsequent rambling answer is blamed for his eventual loss. The lesson is to always have answers available to even the most obvious of questions.

Memorizing important answers

Before you interact with the public, have an answer to the following questions:

> Why are you running?

> Why should I or anyone else vote for you?

» How do you label yourself politically?

» What do you plan to accomplish?

» Why are you better than your opponent(s)?

Media trainers recommend that you have three answers to each question. The first is the short one — say, 5 seconds. Then you have a 15-second answer. The final answer is less than one minute.

TIP

Always get to the point. Be concise. I've seen plenty of amateur candidates blather on and bore everyone. Most people stop listening after 5 seconds, unless you're extremely entertaining or just a weirdo. Don't prattle.

Avoiding awkward answers

People love to talk. I'm guessing that you're a person, which means you probably enjoying talking and could do so endlessly. That's the nature of politicians. It's also something people dislike about politicians.

When you answer a question, don't open with an attack, even if it's valid. Focus on yourself and your position.

If enticed to address your opponent's comments or missteps, refocus the issue immediately. "My campaign is about looking to the future, not the past." Or, "Mr. Skeezeball can address those issues on his own time. I'm here to talk about my campaign."

Don't get into the weeds on a topic. If you're a worthy candidate, you've studied the issues and probably know some major deficiencies of the organization or your incumbent opponent. Avoid sharing those specifics in an answer, because it would take too long to get the public up to speed. Say, "I know some important issues the public is unaware of." If they want more details, offer them. As you do, keep your answers short. Don't lecture.

If you don't know an answer, say so. "I didn't know about that, but I'm eager to look into it." Or, you can fib a bit by answering, "I was recently made aware of this issue and still need some time to formulate my response." (Technically, it's not a fib, because "recent" can mean "just now.")

Don't be condescending or patronizing. This issue is more of a concern for incumbents seeking reelection. In fact, if your incumbent opponent comes across as arrogant, whip out an immediate response, if asked: "I would never treat members of the public in that manner."

Election Registration

At some point, stipulated by the election code, you must register as a candidate. This process involves filling in forms and other paperwork, which is tradition because government can't have enough pieces of paper lying about.

>> Registering for the election is different from making an announcement. It's an official act that puts you on the ballot.

>> You want to register for the election after you make your announcement. If you reverse the order, your registration — which is a public document — spoils the announcement. Political busybodies are always watching for people to register for an election. Don't tip your hand.

>> To register, contact the election authority for the political division for which you seek office. This information is easy to find anonymously by browsing the agency's website. Refer to Chapter 7 for information on who runs the election.

Understanding the qualifications for office

Election laws vary from state to state. It's important that you meet these qualifications before you invest any time or money into a campaign.

The qualifications include

>> **Residency:** You must be a resident in the district you plan to represent. You can't just own property there — you must have a full-time residence or primary residence.

>> **Time in the district:** Not only is residency important, but you also may be required to have lived in the district for a given amount of time. It could be a few months, a year, or longer.

>> **Age:** Some offices have minimum age requirements.

>> **Other qualifications:** It's not common that you need law enforcement experience to run for sheriff, though it helps. You must, however, be an attorney in your state if you plan to run for a legal office, such as district attorney, prosecutor, or judge. Other offices may have similar restrictions.

If you fail to meet any requirements of office, you won't make it on the ballot. Even worse is when you mess up, or the election's office messes up, and you're unceremoniously removed from the ballot. You don't want that to happen.

Scrutinize the requirements. Your opponents will. And you should scrutinize them as well.

Filing the forms

The most important part of obtaining and filling in the various candidate forms is to get your name correct on the ballot. That's because your legal name may not be the way people recognize you.

For example, my first name is legally Daniel. On the ballot, I appear as Dan because that's how everyone knows me. If your legal name is Parker William Toddington but everyone calls you Todd, ensure that name gets on the ballot this way: Todd Toddington or even P.W. "Todd" Toddington.

You may also be required to register your campaign committee, chairman, or financial treasurer. This registration is required in order to comply with your state's campaign finance laws. Filing this declaration may be a requirement before your campaign can legally raise money.

CAMPAIGN CALENDAR

>> The dates for filing campaign forms should be placed on your campaign calendar.

>> It's possible to declare your candidacy and file the forms to register your campaign committee or treasurer for fundraising purposes well before you officially file for the election. In fact, many candidates do so, which extends the time they can solicit funds.

WARNING

RUNNING AS A WRITE-IN

Here's my succinct advice for running as a write-in candidate: Don't.

When you declare as a write-in, it immediately signals to knowledgeable voters that you're unprepared for the election. Serious candidates study and file on time.

Further, the efforts you must apply to a write-in campaign are monumental compared with running a well-thought-out and planned campaign. Rules vary from state to state, but in some places the voter must write your name exactly as it was registered. Any misspellings invalidate the write-in vote.

If you miss the deadline to be on the ballot, wait until the next election.

Commit Your Time

The final step to preparing your run for office is to dedicate yourself to the task. It's not a part-time gig. It's not limited to nights and weekends. Running for office will become your full-time, primary job.

You must be available to work on the campaign, assist volunteers, answer phone calls, reply to email, attend meetings, beg for money, and spend a lot of time trying to win. The process is all-consuming.

Check any appointments or other obligations you have for the duration of the campaign. You'll be criticized if you can't make a forum or attend a meeting because of a wedding or another event. It's fair criticism, too; the public expects you to be dedicated to the campaign.

Do not go out of town or plan trips away from the campaign. Your opponents will mention your absence and point out that if you were serious, you'd show up to the forum or debate.

>> As with any project, the time commitment becomes greater the closer you get to election day. The final week of the election will be insanely busy for you.

>> Oddly enough, the final weekend may not be so intense. You may do some door-knocking or make phone calls, but most of the campaign is done by then.

>> A marvelous sense of calm comes over all candidates toward the end of the campaign. Whether you feel good or bad, you'll be happy it's ending.

DAN SAYS

>> I know one candidate who skipped town for almost the entire election and won. His circumstances were unique: It was a two-way race and the incumbent was unpopular. The turnout was low, but the voters were motivated to rid themselves of the detested incumbent.

3

The Campaign

Chapter **9**

Gather Your Assets

A political campaign's assets are more than money. Cash doesn't guarantee a victory any more than cheesy online polls that say you're going to win. Money helps, of course, but also important are people, a solid message, and other items valuable to a successful campaign.

» The purpose of campaign assets are to help you win.

» Never discount an asset. Too many people focus only on money, yet having a legion of volunteers, a solid message, and some heavy-hitting endorsements can also boost you to victory.

» Money is covered in Chapter 11. You won't find any money there, but the topic is present.

People to Help You

No candidate wins alone. To build your team, you must convert your family, friends, and supporters into campaign helpers. They become the first of your assets and the most important.

Finding required people

The first required person to run for office is the candidate. Duh. Other people may also be required, per the rules that govern the election. Specifically, you may need to publicly declare a campaign chairman, committee, or treasurer — or a combination of these.

The way to know for certain is to check with the agency running the election. Your candidate's packet (provided by the election authority) tells you which people are required. Forms are provided that you must file, indicating key campaign positions.

Some candidates agonize over who is to be their committee chair or treasurer. They want to pick a well-known name or some individual who brings gravitas. If you feel that way, fine; having a former elected official or well-known community name serve as a committee chair or treasurer is believed to affect voters who may not recognize a candidate's name. But, realistically, few of the voters pay attention to such details.

>> Confirm whether your committee chair or treasurer or other names must appear on all your campaign material. See Chapter 10 for details on your branding efforts.

>> These required people are necessary for transparency. The public wants to know who's behind your campaign.

>> A treasurer may not be necessary for a small election, but having someone other than the candidate handle the money is mandatory for statewide and national elections.

>> If the law allows it, you can act as your own treasurer or campaign finance director.

>> It helps to find a treasurer or committee chair who knows the position and the rules of the election. If not, if you're going for name recognition, ensure that another of your people assets can advise you on filing the financial reports.

>> When key positions are optional, some candidates may declare special people anyway. They place these people on the campaign material for name recognition purposes.

DAN SAYS

>> I've had several people serve as campaign treasurer in my various campaigns. Recently, however, I've become my own treasurer, which makes filing the reports easier. Further, one of my treasurers quit in the middle of a campaign, which caused me to incur extra expense because I was required to update all my marketing material.

NAMING YOUR CAMPAIGN COMMITTEE

It would be fun to name your campaign committee The Smartest People Who Support The Best Candidate For Selectman, Tim Anderson. This name says a lot, but it's also long and contains 12 words. That's too many.

Long committee names occupy a lot of space on your campaign material, which means less room for your messaging. For a classified ad, a long name has a per-word fee. Your ad must have the text *Paid for by The Smartest People Who Support The Best Candidate For Selectman, Tim Anderson."* This cost may seem negligible in the big campaign funding picture, but it adds up.

Short committee names are best: The Committee to Elect Tim Anderson or Tim Anderson Selectman. Brevity is best.

Using a campaign manager

The code may not require you to have a campaign manager, but it helps. This person's purpose is to provide advice and guide your campaign. Ideally, you want someone who knows the local political landscape or has previously run campaigns. They can tell you what to do, and what not to do, and offer suggestions and insights specific to the office you seek.

The best campaign managers have good connections. This person knows people and can make introductions. Even better is when the campaign manager can help organize your marketing material and get things printed. They know who prints quickly and who can get you a discount, and they may even design the material themselves or know a good designer. All this knowledge is worth the price a campaign manager charges.

>> The campaign manager is different from a campaign committee chair, which is a largely ceremonial role.

>> Campaign managers charge you a fee. Most of the money you pay is pass-through — and it's cheaper than paying for some items yourself. Still, the person doing the work must get paid. Never cheat or shaft a campaign manager.

Obtaining other important people

Important people for your campaign include your closest advisors, friends, and family. Call them your *kitchen cabinet.* You need not make formal meetings with these people, but doing so helps build a sense of camaraderie. They provide emotional support for low points and can help cheer you on.

These people are basically your super-volunteers. The campaign committee chair can help organize them. Ensure that you put them to work, assigning jobs as described throughout this part of the book.

DAN
SAYS

>> Your core volunteers and supporters comprise your kitchen cabinet. They should head up tasks for you, lead events, and provide moral support.

>> The term *kitchen cabinet* was a negative term applied to President Andrew Jackson's group of core advisors. These people were not members of his official cabinet. Instead, they were individuals seeking to influence Jackson. The term has changed over the years, losing its negative connotation. President Ronald Reagan had a well-known kitchen cabinet of advisors, consisting mostly of businessmen he knew from California.

Recruiting volunteers

You may have an army of friends, associates, and family members — including sisters and cousins (reckoned by the dozens) and aunts — but you still need more people to act as volunteers. They are a wonderful, necessary resource.

Among your kitchen cabinet or another group of key individuals, designate one as the volunteer coordinator. Ask someone who is good with people and reliable for placing phone calls, and who is a generally positive and upbeat presence.

Work with your volunteer coordinator to locate volunteers. Ask personal friends, business associates, and contacts at your church, social clubs, political groups, and other locations where you've been gregarious.

When recruiting new volunteers, ask only whether they would be willing to help. You may not have specific tasks lined up yet, but you must build the list. If later someone asks, mention that you need help door-knocking, stuffing envelopes, attending events, making phone calls, and so on. Call on your volunteers as you need them.

REMEMBER

>> Don't be afraid to ask someone to volunteer for you. Tell them it's cheaper than writing a check, but still ask them for a check.

>> See Chapter 13 for specific volunteer duties and events.

>> Always thank your volunteers.

Your Message

Your campaign must communicate a message telling the voters about you. It answers some immediate questions and defines you as a candidate. Your message is an important part of your campaign, appearing on your literature and advertising. You've probably seen such messaging from other campaigns. If you've paid attention, you're aware that coming up with a good message is more difficult than it seems.

Honing a message

You know why you're running for office. The purpose of your message is to communicate that reason to the voter. It must be solid, punchy, and true.

To hone your message, write a list of reasons why you're running for office and why people should vote for you. Fill the page. Then prioritize the list to your top three. Don't use more than three; the voter is interested in what you stand for, not in reading a novel.

The first message on the list must be your key issue, the main reason you're running for office. Next come other issues, which might be issues raised by the public or other important matters.

The messages must be tidy. It's an introduction, and it showcases your central campaign issue. For example:

"It's time parents had a voice on the school board."

This example is better than droning on: "For far too long, special interests have controlled the school board, dismissing parent's concerns and refusing to listen . . ." You get the idea.

A good message can be made shorter: "A voice for parents."

REMEMBER

Most people give campaign literature about 3 seconds of their time. To keep them reading, you must have a powerful hook that interests them. Further, your literature, signs, and other material don't have a lot of room for meaningless drivel. See Chapter 10 for information on campaign branding.

>> The key to getting the message right is that you can eventually expand upon it in your literature. The message flows easily into the primary goal you want to accomplish when elected.

>> Three message items are enough.

>> Shun those trite, single-word messages; see the later section "Avoiding meaningless mush."

>> Don't get into small details that the public can't relate to. You may know that the agency's copier contract is overpriced. That's an important issue for you as an elected official, but trivial during a campaign.

>> If you need only one message, and it's powerful, go with that.

Updating your bio

You may already have a biography you use, especially if you've applied to various social organizations or served on government committees. It's time to update that bio or create a new one specific to your campaign.

Your bio serves as an introduction to who you are. It talks about your accomplishments and why you're well-suited for the public position you're seeking, and it mentions your work history and family.

Write different versions of your bio. Create a long one for the press and to put on your website. Write a shorter version to serve as an introduction at public events, to be read by a moderator or fundraiser host. Another version should be brief — just a paragraph. Have all three renditions ready, just in case.

WARNING

Do not lie in your biography. Even the smallest fib serves as cannon fodder for a diligent opponent.

For example, if you didn't graduate from your university, write *attended* instead of *graduated*. Likewise, your work history must be legitimate. If you've only lived in the area 12 years, don't claim 20. Instead, write long-term resident. It's okay to be vague, but if you lie, you've just dropped a notch in the election results.

Chapter 3 offers methods for boosting your public resume, which is a great way to add items to your biography.

Avoiding meaningless mush

Coming up with a good message is difficult. Coming up with a worn message is cinchy. For example, how many times have you seen single words on a candidate's literature, such as

- » Leadership
- » Integrity
- » Independent
- » Honesty
- » Trustworthy

This list goes on, but you get the idea. These single-word slogans are meaningless mush. They don't tell the public anything about you. They're overused. You can do better: Don't waste the opportunity to communicate a valid message, especially if you can get it down to a few words.

DAN SAYS

It seems everyone running for office claims to be a fiscal conservative. They pledge never to vote for any tax increase. The truth is that spending is the real problem, not taxes. Rather than promise *Lower taxes* or use the trite phrase *Cut taxes*, boast that you'll watch spending. Or be bold and claim you'll cut spending. Have some specifics handy because someone will legitimately ask what you're going to cut.

Making promises

As a budding politician, you must know that promises come in two types: those you make and those you keep. The first list is far longer than the second.

It's difficult to make promises you can keep, because most elected positions put you on a board, a legislative body. To keep your promise, you must set an agenda item, get a second on a motion, and persuade a majority of your peers to agree with you. Even when you're successful, this process can take years to accomplish.

Rather than promise, say that you'll *work hard,* and then follow that phrase with the rest of the promise. Say "I promise to bring transparency to the town council," say "I'll work hard to restore transparency to the town council." Whether you work hard is up for debate, but breaking a promise is easy to prove.

Endorsements

An endorsement helps the voter to frame who you are and who supports you. The best endorsements come from well-recognized names, people who are respected in the community. Often, seeing an endorsement on your campaign material is good enough for some voters.

To draw endorsements, you must ask. Rarely does a group seek you out and beg you to meet with them for a sit-down. Even as a popular candidate or incumbent, it's up to you to reach out to various groups and ask for an endorsement.

I recommend that you meet with as many groups as possible during your campaign, which is a good strategy. Be aware that not every group can endorse. Specifically, some nonprofits are prohibited from making political endorsements. Still, meet with them, if you can. Seek out those endorsements.

>> Good groups to reach out to include community service organizations (which won't endorse), the chamber of commerce (which also won't endorse), local contractors, Realtors, civic-minded groups, employee unions and associations, neighborhoods and HOAs, and various activist groups.

>> Set meetings with community leaders and businesspeople, many of whom you'll find at service organizations such as Rotary, Kiwanis, Lions, Elks, and others. Set up 1-on-1 meetings and ask for support.

>> Don't be put off if you fail to receive an endorsement. Especially if you're an unknown quantity, expect some justified hesitation. Be civil if you're rejected. Never hold against someone their refusal to endorse.

>> Endorsements cut both ways. Your endorsement by local Realtors may sit fine with some people, but the slow-growth crowd may view that endorsement as a sellout.

DAN SAYS

>> Beyond an endorsement, you can ask for money but also word-of-mouth. I never received an endorsement or money from a certain bigwig in my town, but he set up a meeting with his peers. I did end up getting money and support from some of them.

Contact Lists

In addition to your campaign calendar (refer to Chapter 8), you must also create some contact lists to help you through the campaign. If you're adept at address book software, consider adding these people to a new category for the campaign:

Volunteers: If you're not fortunate enough to have a volunteer coordinator, that job falls to you. Create the list of volunteers. You may never call on them, but if you need to stuff envelopes, go door-to-door, or obtain moral support, these are the people you call.

Yard sign locations: Keep track of where you plant your yard signs. It's your job to collect them when the campaign is done. If you have a list of people you gave your signs to, you can phone them and ask to pick up and return the signs, or learn their location so that you can finish the job.

Donors: This important list contains people you ask to help fund your campaign. See Chapter 11.

Media: Identify the names of reporters who cover the local election. These include reporters from TV and radio and even bloggers. You must know how they prefer to receive press releases and whether it's okay to phone or text them. Also know their deadlines.

These lists grow as your campaign gets under way. Spending time on the phone is something all candidates do. In fact, get a good headset for your phone, if you don't have one already.

Chapter **10**

Your Campaign Brand

B randing is the reason why most children recognize Ronald McDonald before they recognize the president of the United States. Good branding is why you choose a vacation spot, visit a specific car dealer, or select an ear cleaner. Best of all, evidence of strong branding is that you aren't aware of its use. It works like magic.

Political campaigns also benefit from branding. Smart candidates coordinate their campaign materials with a unified theme. Successful branding can help make your name and message "pop" among the voters.

» The best political branding in recent memory is the *O* logo from Barack Obama's 2008 presidential campaign. It was marketing genius, since imitated but never equaled.

» The most historically successful political brand is the hammer-and-sickle of the Communist party. It instantly broadcasts a message. Designed in 1918 by Yevgeny Kamzolkin, who won a design competition cosponsored by Vladimir Lenin, though as a communist he never collected royalties from its use.

Marvelous Marketing Mavens

Don't try to create your own marketing materials. I'm certain you do wonderful things with Microsoft Paint, or perhaps you have a nephew who's a genius at Adobe Illustrator. Unless you do marketing for a living, the smart move is to hire a marketing consultant to design your campaign materials.

A marketing consultant isn't a campaign manager, though some can do both jobs. What you need is an expert who understands marketing. This person must know messaging and graphic design and have experience in branding. Further, marketing people have connections with advertising people, print shops, and bulk mailers. If you can find one person who can do all that, you're set.

Ideally, find a marketing maven who has experience with political campaigns. This choice is important because finding the right person can save you money on branding, creating printed materials, mailing, and other important projects.

Yes, you must pay the marketing person. The cost is worth it, especially as you start observing opponents who lack solid branding and who have overpaid to have their material produced.

>> Refer to Chapter 9 for information on the campaign manager's role.

>> The campaign manager may have a preferred marketing person, which is yet another reason to hire a campaign manager.

>> Beyond their experience, you're also paying a marketing person to find other people, such as designers and print shops that further save you money.

You Are the Product

Your campaign brand is about more than just how your yard signs look. What you're selling is yourself — your name and you personally. Then comes your message. The goal of your marketing campaign and branding is to present you as a reliable commodity to the voter.

Generating name recognition

You may hear marketing people refer to name recognition as *impressions*. Whenever a voter sees your name during a campaign, that's an impression. Here are some examples:

>> A mailer generates one or two impressions, depending on how many voters reside at that address.

>> An advertisement (not free) or article (free) in the local paper can generate as many impressions as the paper's circulation.

>> A billboard generates impressions equal to the number of cars that drive by daily.

>> Bumper stickers, yard signs, and other campaign propaganda generate impressions for every person who sees them.

These impressions must be coupled with your branding so that your name is recognized. The branding develops an image that instantly communicates who you are, what your issues are, and your qualifications.

When people see those golden arches, they know what to expect. Your goal with name recognition is the same as Ronald McDonald's.

Creating written material

To assist your marketing genius, assemble assets you've already created for your campaign. These were discussed in Chapter 9: Your message, issues, and other themes.

Your campaign material relies on your theme to create text, brochures, handouts, letters to voters, and so on. You must write this material. Your marketing person can edit it for you and offer suggestions, but you must generate something to serve as a base.

To help you, write a page-long letter to a voter. Explain who you are, list your goals and issues, and add a few words about any key opponents. Wrap it up with the reason why voting for you is the best idea since the founding of the country. Don't worry about being wordy; you and the marketing person will hone it later.

From the one letter, you can pull specific items to be added to other campaign material. You modify it, focus it, and fit it to the material's size. The point is that you have the material to work with.

>> Your goal with written material is to connect with the voter. A good campaign marketing person knows all the tricks to help you make that connection.

>> Stay positive.

>> Don't be arrogant. Don't talk down. Don't tell about your astounding success and how much money you have. Be humble.

>> Cite facts where possible, but avoid getting into details that bore your reader.

>> Some mushy statements are worth avoiding as bullet points in your campaign material: *honesty, leadership, trustworthiness,* and other terms say nothing about you. See Chapter 9.

>> Your campaign material also needs a bio. This information is also covered in Chapter 9. •

>> The odds of a voter reading your entire missive decrease proportionally to its length. A good marketing person shows you how to keep the reader engaged.

DAN
SAYS

>> Some campaign advisors say never to mention your opponent's name in your written material. It's good advice because you need not give anyone free advertising. So instead you write "my opponent" or "one of my opponents" or "my chief opponent." In person, however, and in forums and debates, refer to your opponents by first name.

Taking campaign photos

Snapping a few quick selfies with your iPhone won't cut it for campaign photos. Consult with your marketing person about getting a professional headshot done. They may have a person in mind who can take the photos, or they may offer suggestions if you want to take them yourself.

Also look through your photo album. You might find a few useful photos there, especially pictures of you interacting with other people or with family and pets, or doing various activities, such as camping.

CAMPAIGN
CALENDAR

If you lack these photos, start taking them at once! Timing is important if you want quality campaign material. Photos come before text, and both must be ready before the campaign starts. Mark on your campaign calendar when photos are required.

>> Suggestions for taking a headshot include how to pose, what the background should be, camera resolution, lighting, and so on.

>> A solid white background works best for a headshot. Taking your picture before a white wall or even a sheet hanging on the wall allows a photo expert to place your image onto other backgrounds.

>> Whether you're dressed in a suit or casual wear depends on the position you seek and the locale. Some communities demand a level of professionalism for their candidates; others are turned off by it.

>> Having pictures of you interacting with others is important. Pictures of you volunteering, meeting with voters, or speaking at meetings all help frame a picture of you that the public can identify with. Contrast these active images with a picture of you sipping tea alone by the fire. You must show people that you're active and engaged.

>> If you don't want to use your photo (and I'll be blunt — say you're ugly), use a photo of your kids or grandkids. I'm not being cruel: Having a voter say, "You're Ryan's grandmother?" means that your campaign marketing material is working.

>> If you're liberal or left-leaning and running in a district where people love their guns, please don't stage a campaign photo of you holding a gun. It just doesn't work.

Magic Marketing Material

The material you need to run the campaign varies, depending on the number of voters, your opponent, and the campaign budget. You don't control any of these items, but you can prepare campaign material to deal with them in advance.

Building a brand

The first step to making your marketing material is to build a brand. A good marketing person works with you to develop the brand. They'll show you thumbnails and offer ideas. You give feedback. Eventually, you come up with a branding sheet that sets your campaign's design, colors, and other themes.

In Figure 10-1, you see a sample branding sheet for city council candidate Tim Anderson. (The real one would be in color.) The branding sheet sets a style, fonts, colors, and graphics.

Campaign material design is based on the branding sheet. The fonts and colors translate to any printed material, websites, letterheads, business cards, and so on.

>> The key items to get from branding are colors and fonts. Having a graphical element is also good, but not required. Name recognition is key, not a logo.

>> In Figure 10-1, details about the fonts and colors are supplied. This information allows printers and web designers to properly reproduce the brand.

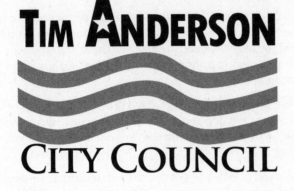

Fonts
Trajan Pro Bold
Tw Cen MT Condensed Extra Bold

Colors	Red	Blue
CYMK	C 0, Y 100, M 100, K 30	C100, Y 80, M 27, K 40
RGB	R 177, G 17, B 22	R 6, G 48, B 90
Web	#B11116	#06305A

FIGURE 10-1: Sample branding sheet.

>> Ask for the Adobe Illustrator or EPS file version of the branding material. You may have to pay extra for this file, though most designers provide it as part of their fee. You can use the file to have printers and others work on your marketing material if the person who designed your branding doesn't perform that task.

>> The more colors you use, the more expensive your campaign material becomes to generate some material. In Figure 10-1, the colors are red and blue with a white background. White is "free" because it's not a color, but the second color (blue or red) adds cost to get materials such as yard signs printed.

>> If you're in a partisan race, branding material may also list your political affiliation.

Creating the traditional handouts

For small districts with low voter turnout, you might get by campaigning door-to-door with some handouts you make and print on your computer. If the district is larger, you need more traditional handouts for your campaign. Two common handouts are business cards and rack cards.

IMPORTANT DETAILS FOR YOUR MARKETING MATERIAL

Confirm your state or local election code for information required to be on your website and all your marketing material and handouts. For example, the law may require that you name your campaign committee or treasurer or other people involved in the campaign. This information must appear in a readable manner as the law stipulates.

The purpose of these disclaimers is to show who supports you or who is funding the campaign. The necessary details are provided in code, but check first, before you print anything. For small material, such as a business card, the information may not be required. The only way to know for certain is to check the law.

Business cards

Use your campaign brand to create standard business cards. Put your name, contact information, and some brief messaging on the card. You want to keep it clean and not wordy. It's a business card, not a manifesto.

TIP

Ensure that you print on both sides of the business card. This approach gives you twice as much space, but it also means your card is always sending a message, no matter how someone holds it.

Cards printed on thick paper stock are great. Cards with raised lettering draw attention. If you want to write on the card, ensure that a finish is used that holds a felt or ink pen.

The number of cards you print depends on the size of the election. Because your goal is to hand out the cards to everyone you meet, print more than you think you need.

TIP

>> An election with low voter turnout would be one with 200 or fewer voters. Even then, going door-to-door may not be practical if the district is rural or covers a large area.

>> A good message to write on a business card is "Sorry I missed you." Then stick the card in the door jamb when going door-to-door.

>> Always hand out your business cards!

Rack cards

A *rack* card is an envelope-sized handout, named such because this type of marketing material usually fits in a rack along with other rack cards, brochures, and trifolds. It's perfect as an envelope-stuffer, handout, or door-knocking handout because it contains just the right amount of printed material.

As with your campaign business card, you print on both sides of the rack card. It's large enough to hold branding, campaign photos, key issues, written material, election information, plus contact information.

If you create a rack card properly, you can even use it as a postcard mailer. In Figure 10-2, you see the rack card mailer format, with ample space to place a stamp and address.

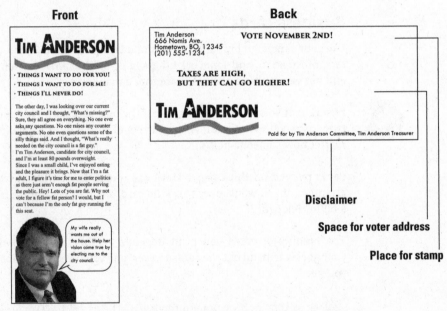

FIGURE 10-2: Configure the rack card as a mailer.

Bring your rack cards to campaign events, fundraisers, or anywhere you've been invited to speak. Set out a few on each table. Hand them out to people who pass by.

Considering other printed material

Beyond letterhead, upon which you can print any letter or press release, your marketing person can help design mailers, yard signs, banners, and billboards. The method of applying these materials is covered in Chapter 12.

PRINTING ADVICE

The puzzle with printing marketing material is that the more you print, the cheaper it costs per unit. Yet you don't want to drive to the recycling station the day after the election and drop off 200 pounds of unused material. So how can you decide how much material to order?

The short answer is that you never know how much printed material you need. The key number is the election turnout, which is a guess, anyway. The second factor is your budget: If you have the money, print the stuff.

I recommend prioritizing items. For anything in an election with over 200 voters in the turnout, business cards are the minimum. If 1,000 voters are anticipated, do rack cards. If you can afford mailers, invest in them as well. If you need more money to cover more material, ask for it. Fundraising is covered in Chapter 11.

It's not important that all these items are designed right away, with perhaps the exception of yard signs, which take a while to produce. Billboards require reservations months in advance. Other items can be generated quickly, providing you have funding.

>> One item to design early might be postcards to send to early voters. You can also use your rack cards as mailers, though if you have the money, a custom postcard targeted to an early voter is best.

>> A good strategy is to send out three direct-mail pieces during the campaign, with two of them arriving during the last two weeks. See Chapter 12 for specifics.

CAMPAIGN CALENDAR

>> If you have a campaign website, get the branding material to your webmaster as soon as possible. The website doesn't need to be up right away, but having it available when you announce your candidacy is a must.

>> Providing you have good branding, and your marketing person has crafted a solid theme, creating your campaign material should be easy. Plus, your campaign then enjoys a consistent, professional look. The voters will notice.

Chapter **11**

Money Stuff

I t's sad but true: Money is the grease that turns the wheels of politics. You wish you didn't have to fund-raise. You prefer not to ask for contributions. Still, money is required if you want to run a campaign. Perhaps you don't need the millions required for a statewide or national office, but money is part of the system at all levels of politics.

» With some low-turnout elections, you might get by raising only a small amount of cash or funding your campaign yourself. Just hope that your opponents don't spend more money.

DAN SAYS

» I've seen campaigns where the incumbents didn't raise any money to win reelection. Generally, they're opposed by people with no name recognition or who are in the race because "no one should run unopposed." Otherwise, everyone must raise money for a political campaign.

Campaign Finances

Your campaign is a short-term, one-goal business. To make it successful, you must be smart about its finances. Part of being an elected official, if not one of your campaign themes, is to watch government spending and control a budget. Start by setting an example with your own campaign.

» You may have a treasurer who manages the campaign money for you, though most local-office candidates manage their own funds.

» If you have a treasurer, ensure that you're closely involved with finances. Insist on being sent reports. Read them. Follow every penny. You don't want sloppy accounting during the campaign to be used against you.

WARNING

» It's imperative that you keep your personal funds and campaign funds separate. Campaign spending is only for legitimate campaign expenses. The laws in your state or locality spell out exactly what is allowed and what is prohibited.

Creating a spreadsheet

Like any business, your campaign must monitor income and expenses. Items must be input with dates, names, and types of expenses. You need to know your cash on hand. You also need to have a budget that shows upcoming expenses, desired projections for income, and items you want if the funding comes through.

Yeah, it's a lot of work.

Many candidates keep track of their campaign's income and expenses in a spreadsheet. They also use the spreadsheet for budgeting. If you're adept at Excel or Google Sheets, that's about all you need.

Craft a simple general ledger in the spreadsheet. Track your expenses on one page, receipts on another, budget on a third. If the campaign finance laws require specific details, ensure that you add them as required.

» If you have a money management program you enjoy, you can use it for your campaign. However, if you don't currently use such software, it makes no sense to learn new software in addition to all the other demands on your time.

» Using professional-level business software such as QuickBooks is a bit much for a local-office run, especially if you lack any paid employees.

>> The election law may require that you enter the names and addresses of people who donate money. Further, you may have to track multiple donations to ensure that certain campaign contribution limits aren't exceeded.

>> It's not necessary to surrender your campaign spreadsheet's data to your opponents or the press. Only the required campaign finance reporting forms are available for public scrutiny. Even then, not every election falls under campaign finance reporting laws.

Receiving cash and checks

Over the course of your campaign, people throw money at you. Not in the manner you think, but if you do your fundraising job (covered later in this chapter), your campaign will receive cash and checks. To best deal with this revenue, as well as to best handle expenses, open a bank account for your campaign.

Many banks and credit unions offer low-cost or free accounts, which is perfect for your campaign. Don't open a business account, because fees are involved. What you seek is a free account that features checking and a debit card.

Name the account after your campaign. Ensure that this name appears on your checks and debit card. Doing so ads a level of professionalism. Supporters may prefer to write their donation checks to a committee as opposed to you personally.

WARNING

>> Do not comingle your campaign funds and private funds.

>> Some vendors may take payments only by credit or debit card.

>> Avoid getting a campaign credit card. You can manage your electronic payments with a debit card just as easily as with a credit card. The goal is to pay off your debts immediately. With a credit card, you may be tempted to let the payments roll over from month to month, which incurs fees.

>> Yes, some donations will have your personal name on the check. This common mistake doesn't imply that the money is yours to keep.

REMEMBER

>> Money received for your campaign isn't yours personally. It's sad that I must write this reminder, yet too many people who run for office seem to think they can do anything they want with campaign donations. Some of these people serve time in prison when they forget the difference.

Taking in-kind donations

Not every contribution to your campaign comes in the form of cash or checks. The *in-kind* contribution is a combined income and expense. It's a donation of services or other items that would otherwise cost the campaign money.

As an example, a local bar hosts a campaign event and donates the meeting room and complimentary food and beverages. These items have a cost to your campaign, which the vendor waives. Your campaign credits itself the cost as a donation but also debits itself the same amount as an expense:

	Donation	Expense
Steve's Bar, room & host		$580.00
Steve's Bar	$580.00	

The election laws in your state or locality offer specifics on how to specify an in-kind donation in your campaign finance reports. In your campaign's spreadsheet, add the in-kind amount as a donation and subtract it as an expense.

>> It's not always possible to get exact pricing on some in-kind donations. A fundraiser at a private home may have homemade goodies and snacks available. Whether to count them as an in-kind donation is a minor quibble. For large-ticket items, such as the donation of a billboard in town, specifying the in-kind donation/expense is a must.

>> In-kind donations are a great way to get funding from supporters who may be reluctant to donate cash directly to your campaign. See the later section "Working through a rejection."

Getting online payments

Before you announce your campaign, set up online payments using one of the available funding sources. For example, I've used PayPal for past campaigns.

Work through the setup instructions on the donation website. Specify that you're running a political campaign; you are not a nonprofit. Supply the campaign information, such as your bank account for transfers.

Have your web designer configure the campaign website with a Donate button. Put the button in an obvious place. Better, put the Donate button all over the site. If someone wants to support you, don't make finding that Donate button into a game of hide-the-thimble.

>> Jot down in your campaign calendar a deadline for setting up online payments.

>> For a small election — say, fewer than 200 voters — you can get by without online donations (or a website, for that matter).

>> You can use the online payment source to pay vendors, but my advice is to transfer the donation directly into your campaign bank account.

>> If the online payment source collects a fee, you must count only the income received as a donation. For example, if someone donates $50.00 but you receive only $47.50, the latter value is the donation.

>> The fee these online payment sources charge is one reason I downplay online donations in my campaigns. If possible, try to collect the money directly as cash or a check.

Setting your funding goal

An experienced campaign manager can spot you a reliable ballpark figure of what your campaign costs — specifically if you do everything right. Doing everything right means generating enough marketing material and mailers to make a lasting impression with the voters. I don't know of any single campaign that's ever achieved this goal.

If you don't have a campaign manager, data is available for you to set funding goals.

The first place you should look are the financial reports from prior elections for the same office. If two years ago the school board trustees spent an average of $4,000 each on their campaigns, that's your goal — or higher.

Turnout is the key to funding an election. Your marketing campaign must reach all the chronic voters and special interests you plan to target. I would multiply the tally of chronic voters by $3 each to set a good funding goal. This rate means if your voter list shows 4,000 regular votes, $12,000 will run you a good campaign. If you want to reach more voters, you spend more money.

Don't be discouraged! The key is not the amount of money you must raise, but rather how wisely you spend it. Some candidates raise a lot of money, but they fritter it away with bad timing or horribly designed material. Remember that elections are decided by who gets the most votes, not by who spends the most campaign money.

TIP

>> Also see the later section "Discovering how much things cost."

>> Stay flexible in your campaign fundraising goal. Prioritize those items that reach the maximum number of voters in the most impactful way.

>> Data disclosing spending from an election is a public record. You request this information from the same authority that runs the election for your district. If you're fortunate, it's free and available instantly online.

>> Ensure that you have a solid voter list for your mailings. Refer to Chapter 7 for information on obtaining and refining this list, as well as how to create a list of chronic voters.

DAN SAYS

>> There's no definitive answer for how much money you must raise, nor that you must outspend your opponent to win. I won my first race spending far less than what my opponent raised.

Money to Spend

It takes no skill to spend money. No university offers a degree. Few can legitimately lay claim to the title of the best money-spending person ever. Your campaign will spend money. How much depends on how much you can raise. The priority is to spend the money wisely.

Discovering how much things cost

Before you set the campaign budget, you must know how much things cost. Even before you decide on a campaign strategy, figuring how best to reach people must be prioritized.

Your marketing person can provide you with a list of what various campaign materials cost: business cards, rack cards, yard signs, mailers, and so on. These prices will be lower than what you'd pay if you produced the material yourself. Remember, marketing people have connections.

For media advertising, obtain a *rate card*. This handy sheet tells you how much advertising costs in the newspaper, discount circulars, radio, and so on.

As an example, a newspaper may have specific rates for given ad sizes, color ads, classified ads, and specific placement in the paper. They may offer special deals for campaigns.

For your mailing, standard first-class mail has a given rate. Add the cost of printing the letter and the cost of the envelope. Hopefully, you get volunteers to help you stuff and address the letters.

If you choose a direct mail outfit, you save money on postage. Further, they may print letters, create postcards, stuff envelopes, and use your voter lists to address your material. The per-unit cost might be better for you, especially in an election with a large turnout (say, more than 10,000 voters). Do keep in mind, however, that the post office doesn't prioritize direct mail.

Compare the cost of first-class mailing with bulk mailing before you make a decision on which to go for. Get quotes from the bulk mailing houses. Your marketing person may offer suggestions on who is best to work with, or they may handle the bulk mailing themselves.

TIP

REMEMBER

>> See Chapter 10 for details on finding a marketing person.

>> In many states, it's illegal for media (newspapers, radio, TV) to boost advertising rates during a campaign season.

>> If you're early, you can get the best placement for your ads in the paper. The same goes for online advertising on a newspaper's website.

>> Direct mail is the same as bulk mail, or junk mail. Use it early. Toward the end of your campaign, sending out material that arrives before the election is important.

>> The first-class mailing rate for a postcard is cheaper than for a standard letter. Size and thickness limits apply to postcard mailings, yet using a postcard is a good way to send out material inexpensively.

GEOFENCING

A new item that newspapers and other media may entice you with is *geofencing*. This form of online advertising is targeted to specific online audiences at given locations. The idea is that your ad shows up as people browse the web — say, when they're waiting to pick up their kids at school or standing in line at the grocery store.

Though geofencing is a fascinating technology, it's effectiveness for a local campaign is dubious. Most people dismiss online ads without reading them. The effectiveness of an online ad on a mobile device is in doubt. Further, the fees associated with geofencing are high when compared with advertising rates offered on social media. See Chapter 12.

Wasting money

A political campaign is about marketing, but it's not the same as a traditional marketing campaign. If you apply a traditional marketing approach to your campaign, you waste money *and* hand an advantage to your opponent.

The best way to spend money on a campaign is to spend it late. The closer to election day, the more valuable every dollar you spend. That's because a typical voter doesn't pay attention to a campaign until just before they vote.

It's also tempting to spend money on things that won't do anything to get you elected. Avoid spending money on buttons, bumper stickers, hats, pencils, balloons, T-shirts, and other baubles.

Don't rent a billboard. For the cost, you could reach hundreds of voters with direct mail or put an ad in the newspaper or on the radio. Just about anything is more effective than a billboard.

Avoid spending money on polling. Yours isn't a race for Congress. Polling is an expensive luxury.

If the item in question is donated as an in-kind expense, go for it. Campaign workers love buttons, hats, and T-shirts. In fact, if you can get volunteers to pay $20 for T-shirts that cost you $5 each, it's a fundraiser. But for spending real campaign dollars, avoid the swag.

>> Your campaign may be 15, 12, or 10 weeks long or shorter. Regardless, and setting aside all the work you do, the voter has a short memory. Sending them material too early is like not sending anything at all.

>> Ignore online polls about your race. Anyone can stack an online poll, and lots of paid and private hacks do just that.

>> Spending one dollar eight weeks before an election is like spending a nickel. Spending that same dollar the week before an election is like spending fifty dollars. The difference lies in the impact your material has on the voter.

>> If your opponent prints T-shirts and offers other tchotchkes, smile. It's to your advantage that they waste money.

DAN SAYS

The Secret to Raising Money

For a small number of politicians, asking for money is no big deal. They're very good at it. For the majority, asking for money is embarrassing and awkward. It seems dirty, especially in a culture that appreciates entrepreneurs and self-made millionaires. Yet the secret to raising money is to ask, and ask you must.

>> Keen political observers note that it's not the total you raise but the number of people contributing. Compare getting one hundred $5 donations with getting five $100 donations. Who has wider support?

>> Asking for money doesn't make you a whore. Receiving money in exchange for promised services does.

Doing background work

Before you ask for a campaign donation, become knowledgeable about the campaign finance limitations for the election. Every state has a cap on the amount of money an individual can donate to a candidate. It's a maximum you cannot legally exceed.

Once you know the maximum limit, prepare a list of donors, organized by those you believe can give you the most money. Call this first crop of supporters the *whales* because they represent potentially large donations.

Prioritize the donor list by those who can support you with a large, but perhaps not the maximum, donation. After contacting potential large supporters, move down the list to others you feel can donate generously. Eventually you start calling the small donors. Of course, all this effort is guesswork; you never know who will write you a large check until you ask.

>> The campaign donation limits may be annual or per election. If they're *per election,* you can receive money in both the primary and general elections for a partisan office. If they're *annual,* you can ask for money the year before you run — if you plan that far ahead.

>> The campaign donation limit usually applies to individuals, not families. It's possible to obtain double the maximum from a couple, for example.

>> Minimum limits may also apply for reporting purposes. For example, donations under $25 may not require you to supply the donor's name on your campaign finance reports. Ensure that you know the rules as set by your state or the election authority.

>> Some smaller districts may not have campaign donation limits or even any form of campaign finance reporting.

>> Refer to Chapter 9 for information on building your donor list.

Asking for money

People donate because you ask.

To fund your campaign, you must ask for money. You make calls daily. You do it right away. You don't put it off. Ask. Ask. Ask.

If you have people who make large donations (see the preceding section), visit them in person. Schedule an appointment. After all, if you want to get a $1,000 or $500 donation from an individual, ask them face-to-face.

For other donors, make calls. Have a list of people you call daily. Leave a message if they don't answer, "This is Tim Anderson; sorry I missed you. I'll try again later." That's it. Otherwise, you make your pitch.

Be positive, solid, and convincing. Fundraising experts claim that you should ask like this:

"I would like you to help support my campaign." Wait for their answer. Because the donor is on your list and you know they're a supporter, it would be unusual for them to say no. (See the later section "Working through a rejection" on the unlikely chance they do say no.)

Next, make the "ask:" "Would you like to donate $500?"

If you hear "Yes," thank them profusely. Otherwise, drop the donation a notch: "How about $250?" And then keep working down: $200, $100, $50. Always ask high and go low. Donors know what they can afford.

What you don't want to do is ask for $50 when the donor may be willing to offer $250. They'll agree to the $50, assuming that you don't need any more. This logic is why you start high and go low.

You must set aside time daily to make these calls. Work through your donor list. This method is how the professionals operate, both politicians and nonprofits. It works.

>> Plan on spending half your campaign time raising money.

>> Go big with the ask.

>> The candidate makes the call. It's not your campaign treasurer's job to ask for money. The ask must come from you, the candidate.

>> Mark down times for donation calls on your campaign calendar. Have one of your supporters check on you to ensure that you're making the calls.

CAMPAIGN CALENDAR

Working through a rejection

Not everyone who supports you may be able to provide your campaign with a cash donation. Conversely, someone you might believe would support you, or may have said positive things to you in the past, is an ardent supporter of your opponent. Don't let such turns discourage you.

TIP

DONATIONS TIPS AND SUGGESTIONS

Have you ever received a donation envelope from a politician? Did you use it? I don't. Often I peel off the stamp and call it a profit.

Donation envelopes don't work as well as phone calls because they involve zero effort. A phone call is personal. A visit is even more personal. These methods work far more successfully than sending out donation envelopes.

If you want to send out donation envelopes, do so for the people you've already met or spoken with who have promised a donation. Send them a thank-you note with a stamped return envelope.

Don't worry if a supporter is slow to write the check. For example, if you make the call on Tuesday, don't expect the check to arrive on Thursday. It might, but most people wait to write checks. This reason is why it's important to ask early, especially for people you suspect will donate the most money.

Always follow through. Send personal thank-you notes to everyone who donates over a certain amount. For me, it's $100. When I receive a donation for $100 or more, I send out a thank-you card. For larger donations, I hand-write a thank-you letter. This attention to detail is exactly why your donors are supporting you.

Be respectful when someone declines a donation. Thank them for offering their time. Explain that you respect and understand their decision. You don't want to close the door; keep the line of communications open.

Providing they don't openly proclaim support for your opponent, ask if they can help in other ways: a donation of time, food, meeting space, or other in-kind donations.

Don't forget the importance of word-of-mouth. Invite them to attend a fundraiser. Ask them if they could help spread the word. Turn the rejection into something positive. Doing so may not turn you into a politician, but it brings you one step closer to being a diplomat.

Strategies for Fundraising

Beyond asking individuals for money, you must supplement your campaign with other sources of income. The most obvious one is the traditional meet-and-greet fundraiser. Less obvious avenues for obtaining donations are available, all of which are legal.

Putting on a meet-and-greet

A meet-and-greet event has two purposes. The first is to meet the voters. This technique works as it forms a lasting impression. The second purpose is to raise funds.

A successful meet-and-greet must be set up weeks in advance. Contact the host, who can be one of your volunteers or another supporter. Ask them to put on a neighborhood event. Provide them with as much support as you can, such as creating flyers or posting on social media. If possible, walk the neighborhood with your supporter to rally plenty of people to attend.

The host is responsible for providing snacks and drinks. You should offer to provide some as well, though most hosts are happy to provide the goodies. Ensure that plenty of campaign material is available to hand out as your host goes door-to-door.

To the event you bring campaign material and yard signs. Bring a basket or tray into which people can place donations. You might even "prime the pump" by placing some money in the basket. If you have donation envelopes, set them in the basket, though any small envelope will do.

During the event, be social. Ensure that you meet everyone. Be cheerful and positive. Remember people's names. Practice your small talk.

At some point you'll be asked to make a statement or prepare a speech. Be short and sweet with your message, and then open for questions.

Ensure that you thank everyone for coming. Above all, thank the host.

>> Not everyone donates at a meet-and-greet, mostly because many people are not political and don't understand that a donation is part of the deal.

>> Avoid knocking any opponents. Don't say anything you don't want repeated. These are voters, not a group of intimate friends. If you say something stupid, it may get out.

>> Technically, the full cost of the meet-and-greet is an in-kind donation. It's up to the host to report the money spent, which you can ask for, but they may not provide it.

>> You must report any donations made during the event in accordance with the campaign finance rules for the election.

>> Cash donations in the basket are difficult to track, which can be an issue if the pot is quite large. I recommend dividing the total amount of donations by the number of attendees and state that amount on the campaign's financial forms.

>> Refer to Chapter 9 for information on honing your message.

Visiting organizations

Ensure that you ask to appear at organizations to share your campaign message. Not every organization — specifically, nonprofits — can donate to a political campaign. Still, you want to get your message out. Every group you can meet with is a plus.

One reason to visit specific organizations, such as a group of Realtors, builders, unions, or associations, is to obtain their endorsement. When you ask to meet with such groups, ask whether they plan to endorse someone in your election. You don't need to ask about a donation; the endorsement often comes with the donation.

>> Work in advance to set up meetings with various groups. These groups rarely reach out to candidates, so you don't want to discover that they've already held candidate interviews and made endorsements.

>> A donation isn't always coupled with an endorsement.

>> Some organizations may offer volunteers instead of endorsing. For example, members may volunteer to go door-to-door or do a literature drop for you.

>> Negatives can be associated with organizations endorsing you. It's legitimate for opponents to claim donations from such groups are "special interest money" or that you're "in the pocket" of such groups. Be prepared to deal with such attacks ahead of time.

Funding yourself

Election and campaign finance laws differ from state to state, but in most places it's perfectly legal to fund yourself. Campaign contribution limits may apply to you or they may not. And you might also be able to make your campaign a personal loan.

On the positive side, a donation to your own campaign is seen as a sign that you believe in yourself. Many political observers view a campaign loan, essentially seed money, as a good thing. It shows you have skin in the game.

On the negative side, do not completely fund your campaign. Many candidates do so because they don't want to seem beholden to special interests (or so they claim), but the truth is that people don't like asking for money. Yet, ask you must.

>> Some millionaires completely self-fund and they're successful. This practice is known as "buying yourself a seat." I've never seen it work at the local level, but statewide and nationally, it happens frequently.

>> Campaign loans are supposed to be paid back through other donations. Even so, because most campaigns never raise enough money, you may end up closing your campaign with a debt — even if you win.

DAN SAYS

>> I've always loaned money to my own campaigns. I've never paid myself back at the end of the campaign. Each one has been closed in debt.

Finance Reports

In most states, campaign finance reports are called *sunshine* reports. The laws governing election finances are likewise called *sunshine* laws. This cheerful term implies that all campaign funding is out in the open. The public must know who is donating money to campaigns and how candidates are spending that money. Let the sun shine.

Knowing the law

The number of laws surrounding election finance seem to grow every year. That's because some bastard out there always figures out a clever way around them — or so he thinks. To be a good candidate, you must know and obey all the rules about election finance, fill in and file reports, and be as honest as a politician can be.

CAMPAIGN CALENDAR

Update your campaign calendar with due dates for your campaign finance reports. These reports cover specific campaign funding periods. You report on income and expenses over the period and then file the reports by the dates required.

If you've kept a spreadsheet, as mentioned at the start of this chapter, filling in the reports is a matter of adding up and copying figures. You don't have to submit your spreadsheets or the campaign budget (nor would you want to), only supply the totals or other information required on the campaign finance forms.

Your key resource in knowing the rules is the election authority. It may be a county organization, such as the registrar of voters, election supervisor, or county clerk. The political subdivision where you're seeking office might also run the election. However it works out, they are the authority for the campaign finance laws. They are the people you should ask when you have questions.

>> Some small-district elections may be exempt from the requirement to submit campaign finance reports. This liberty mustn't be interpreted as saying you can play fast and loose with campaign funding. Always keep a spreadsheet of campaign income and expenses. If you want to be truly transparent, publish the information yourself and challenge your opponents to do likewise.

>> Contributions to your political campaign are not taxable as income under state and federal law. They're considered donations, exempt from taxation. Even so, check your state's election finance laws to ensure that donations are exempt from income tax.

>> Don't be shy about asking questions about campaign finance, and don't avoid getting help filling in the reports. Even when you're the outsider, the staff who run the election are there to help you. Take advantage of their assistance if you need it.

>> Read your opponent's forms because they will read yours. You can see where their donations are coming from and gauge their type of campaign by how they're spending money.

DAN SAYS

>> Political strategists claim that you should turn in your financial reports on the day they're due, even if you have them ready early. It's a funny game they play, not wanting to be first. I've never paid attention to these games. Especially if I've done a good job of raising money, I turn in my reports early for the world to see.

Dealing with campaign finance problems

Two important traditions in this country are performed by amateurs: weddings and local-office political campaigns. Goof-ups at a wedding can be dreadful or hilarious but without lingering consequences. Screw up your campaign finance report and the vultures drool.

Mistakes happen. A simple math error is forgivable. If possible, try to correct it. Hopefully, the agency collecting your financial reports will spot any errors and offer you a chance to correct them or amend the report.

A bigger problem than not properly totaling a column or copying a figure is submitting your campaign finance report late. Some states may fine you for each day it's late. Your opponents and other political detractors will dance and squeal like their hair is on fire after such flubs.

The best way to deal with any problem in a campaign finance report is to address it immediately. Have the elections official or clerk help you remedy the situation. If necessary, address the problem with a press release. Only your opponents care about such flubs, and the hay they make won't feed any horse.

>> Report your campaign mistakes at once.

>> If your opponent nitpicks a mistake in your finance reports, let it go. Such issues are considered trivial by the voters, and perhaps even a sign of desperation.

>> Accordingly, if you notice mistakes in your opponent's campaign finance reports, let them go. Unless someone is hiding a lot of money or you have solid proof of wrongdoing, the local press will do a better job of reporting it than your campaign will.

- » **Mailing campaign literature**
- » **Planting yard signs**
- » **Knocking on doors**
- » **Debating your opponents**
- » **Creating press releases**
- » **Deciding to go negative**
- » **Defending yourself**

Chapter **12**

Communications

A campaign is a battle fought with ideas. To be successful in that battle, you must effectively communicate your ideas to the voter. Get enough of them to agree with your message, remember your name, and mark your spot on the ballot, and you win.

Connect with Your Audience

"Did you hear that the Prince of Wales will be the next King of England?" said no one in the UK ever. That's because the British know the royals and the line of succession. Minus a few historical surprises, the players are obvious.

In the United States, no one knows you're running for local office until you announce. Not everyone will be aware you're running even as you're doing so. A clutch of voters may not know an election is being held until the day before.

Therefore, the first goal of campaign communications is to connect with your audience.

>> This section assumes that you have already crafted a message and have branding in place. If not, refer to Chapter 10.

>> Refer to Chapter 7 for information on how to discover who votes in an election.

>> Refer to Chapter 11 for details on setting up meet-and-greets and scheduling appointments to meet with various organizations.

Using social media

Without a doubt, a social media presence during a campaign helps increase your exposure to the voters. The big question is social media's relevance in a small race: Will it affect the outcome?

The good news is that social media is well-known and incurs only time as an expense. It costs nothing to set up accounts on Twitter, Instagram, Facebook, and similar sites. Once you have an account, and have populated it with interesting material, place your social media contact details in your marketing material.

The key to attracting visitors to your social media account is to generate new material. For example, four posts per day to Facebook would be required to match the pace at which most people access the site. Multiple daily tweets about your campaign are necessary. The occasional video and campaign photo upload also help. The more active you are, the more successful the social media campaign becomes.

TIP

>> If you plan to set up advertising on Facebook, you must start early. Facebook requires a verification process that can take weeks to complete. Details may change later, but at the time this book goes to press, you must provide proof of who you are and a physical address before you can run a political advertisement on Facebook.

>> Social media advertising is relatively inexpensive, though whether it's effective for a local race is unknown.

>> Always be positive online. Engage with people, but leave it up to your supporters to do battle with the online trolls. See the nearby sidebar, "Do not engage the trolls."

>> Unless you already have a campaign website available, or you can get one done quickly and inexpensively, I don't recommend it. Campaign websites lack the expediency of social media. To best connect with the voter, use Twitter,

Facebook, and other sites, which the public checks with far more frequency than a campaign website.

» Videos are a great way to communicate with the voter. Make them short and direct. If you have a volunteer who knows video production and can assist you, all the better.

» You may find that social media is a good tool for your fans but has little effect in convincing others to support you.

» Don't bother comparing Facebook likes between your own site and an opponent's. Likes come from anywhere, including your relatives, friends, co-workers, and others who live outside the district and cannot vote in your election.

Sending direct mail

Yes, *direct mail* is another term for *bulk mail*, disparagingly referred to as *junk mail*. It's the most effective method to reach the voter — especially if you've honed your voter lists, as recommended in Chapter 7.

Based on your lists, you can craft several mailers to send out. Ideally, you want to send out three:

» An introduction

» An ongoing-campaign info piece

» A final, get-out-the-vote reminder

WARNING

DO NOT ENGAGE THE TROLLS

It's difficult to sit back while some jerk attacks you online. You may not even know him. Though such a person is soulless, they have a purpose: to entice you to anger. Upon success, they share your comments with their friends, gloating over their success at having irked a candidate for public office. (I wonder what these people did for fun before the Internet?)

Avoid at all costs engaging anyone you don't know in an online debate. Your best — and *only* — response must be, "I would enjoy speaking with you about this issue. Please contact me so that we can sit down and chat." Offer your phone number or email address. And don't worry: They won't call you, because a discussion isn't their goal. Beware the trolls.

These pieces can be letters, cards, fold-outs, or brochures. Send out as many pieces as you can afford — ideally, your entire chronic-voter list every time and maybe more. If you have more funds, send out additional mailers or widen the list of voters.

Options for mailers

Common campaign mailers include postcards (which can be larger than the traditional vacation postcard size), letters, trifolds, and large envelopes.

The larger the item, the more it costs per unit to send. On the other hand, the larger the item, the more material you provide to the voter.

What to include

The first mailer must be your introduction. Talk about who you are and your issues.

Start with a hook, such as stating a well-known or commonly perceived issue you plan to resolve:

> *Everyone talks about growth. Our population is on the rise, and town services are struggling to match the pace. The public would like to see more action on this topic, but our Town Council appears more interested in appeasing development than responding to the concerns of citizens living here now.*

Follow the hook with your introduction, validating why you're the ideal person to solve this issue:

> *I'm Tim Anderson, long-time resident and concerned citizen. I'd like to see more action from our council. After years of trying, I've decided to take my talent and expertise and run for office. My goal is to represent you and other people who are tired of being ignored by our elected officials.*

Explain how you'll be different from your opponent(s) without using any names or resorting to personal attacks:

> *My opponent is a two-term incumbent who has always sided with more development — let's be honest — sprawl. I've tried to speak with him on this issue, but his mind is closed.*

Wrap it up, staying positive:

> *I will do better to represent you. I hear the needs of the citizens. Beyond controlling growth, we need to increase response times for our police department, and we must hold the line on spending*

> *It's time for a change in City Hall. I look forward to your support and your vote in November.*

Keep it simple and short. My example is okay for a letter, but it could be better. Ensure that others read it over and offer input and suggestions.

Avoid getting into too many specifics that a typical voter would find boring. For example, don't do this:

> *Ten years ago, the percentage of the village's general fund supplied through property tax was 34.5 percent, supplemented by state tax and sales tax funding. Since Mayor Hamilton's spending spree, the property tax percentage has ballooned to 51.2 percent, an increase of nearly 150 percent on the backs of the taxpayers.*

Instead, say this:

> *Taxes are ever increasing with no end in sight.*

Depending on your budget, you may need to pare down your message. Be prepared to condense.

For your second piece, offer more information as prepared in your marketing material. Highlight yourself and what you plan to do. Explain how the public will be better served by you as opposed to your opponent(s).

The final piece must urge citizens to get out and vote. This piece has the most impact because it happens late in the campaign, when more people are paying attention. Ensure that your message and other items of importance are properly expressed.

REMEMBER

>> If you've never written such a letter before, ensure that you have plenty of others read it over and offer input.

>> Voters may give your material a cursory glance before throwing it in the trash or recycle bin. You must attract and keep their attention. This process is aided when you have a good marketing person on your team. See Chapter 10.

>> Also see the later section "To Go Negative."

What to always include

All direct-mail pieces must include the following information, in order of importance:

Disclosures required per election code: Direct-mail pieces in most elections require a notice of the campaign committee, treasurer, or other data. Do not forget this detail!

Your name and contact information: Your name must appear on both sides of the mailer. Contact information is required for mailing, but also for the public if they want to get in touch with you. Include both your phone number and email address.

The office you seek: Be specific. If you're running to represent a specific district, ward, or seat, put it on the material.

The election date: You know the election date, but most voters haven't committed it to memory. Remind them.

Absentee information: Especially for early material, or mail you target to absentee voters, provide details for how to vote absentee, where to obtain the ballot, how to register, and so on.

TIP

If you can afford it, include an absentee ballot application in your initial mailer. This addition can be expensive, and you must confirm with the election authority that you can send out such material.

How to send the mailer

The simplest way to produce the mailer is to print the material yourself, address each item, and apply postage. For mailing up to 1,000 units, this approach works, especially when the campaign has eager volunteers.

For a larger mailing, printing and mailing can be done separately or together.

For example, you can have your marketing person obtain a good rate to print several thousand units of a postcard mailer. Then you can have an addressing-and-stamping party for your volunteers.

An alternative is to have everything printed, addressed, and mailed by a bulk mailing house. Your marketing person should have connections in the area to provide you with several alternatives. The mailing house can give you a quote, which you can run through your campaign budget to determine whether it's a better option.

The advantage of bulk mail is that everything is done for you: printing, addressing, and mailing at the bulk rate. They can even massage your voter list. The disadvantage is that the material may not be printed with the same quality you'd get elsewhere, and the post office doesn't prioritize delivery of bulk mail.

Making some yard signs

It may be different elsewhere, but where I live, people believe that yard signs are the number-one tool you need to win an election. Poppycock.

Yard signs are a good way to spread your campaign brand, have supporters show their enthusiasm, and make your opponents nervous. But by themselves they don't win elections.

>> Invest in yard signs as part of your campaign strategy.

>> Don't bother counting your opponent's yard signs, because elections are won by votes and not the number of yard signs littering lawns and highways.

>> Check with the rules of your region with regard to yard sign placement. For example, you may be prohibited from setting a yard sign on public property in the public right-of-way.

>> Yard signs may also require a permit in some jurisdictions. Make a note when the permit allows you to set out — and remove — yard signs on your campaign calendar.

>> Yard sign wars are a real thing. They're a great example of how even a local, nonpartisan election can rack up the immaturity points on both sides: Your opponent's supporters will damage and steal your yard signs. They will stick their yard signs one inch in front of yours. They will illegally place their yard signs. And your supporters may do the same things to the other yard signs. Just let it go. Yard sign wars don't win campaigns, and complaining about stolen yard signs makes you come across as desperate.

CAMPAIGN
CALENDAR

DAN
SAYS

Philosophy

Yard signs are about name recognition. The sign's design should be tied to your campaign branding. A car driving by at 35 MPH should be able to identify your campaign based on the yard sign, which is yet another impression in the minds of the voter.

On a practical level, yard signs are pretty much for supporters. They make wonderful handouts for meet-and-greet events. People are proud to show whom they've voting for, and having a yard sign makes them happy.

I provide yard signs primarily for my supporters. Rarely, if ever, is the sight of a yard sign the deciding factor in someone voting for you or, better, switching over from voting for your opponent. Otherwise, I don't believe yard signs have any impact on the election whatsoever.

Availability

For a typical local election, print about 100 yard signs per 2,000 potential voters. If you run out, you can print more. Have them available always, ready for supporters. If you can organize volunteers to set yard signs, hand them a bunch and let them have at it — after fully informing them of the various yard sign rules and regulation. See the later section "Placement."

Let other supporters know where they can pick up a yard sign. Specifically, send them to various meet-and-greet events to obtain one. That way, you draw more attendance at such events.

Details

Yard signs are about campaign branding. The key element is your name. You can also add the position you seek. Required are any disclaimers, such as the campaign committee, treasurer, or other legally required details that must be printed on all your campaign material.

A typical yard sign measures 24-by-18 inches. Larger sizes are available, though you should check the restrictions on yard sign sizes for your locale.

The traditional yard sign is printed on a coated cardboard material. It's weather resistant. Don't go cheap and get a noncoated yard sign, because it will fade and flop in the weather.

One important part about the yard sign is the mounting mechanism. Most signs are mounted on wires stuck into the ground. Called *H-wires*, these have an additional cost beyond the yard sign expense. Larger yard signs may require you to purchase wooden stakes or other methods to mount the signs.

Yard sign do's and don'ts

Keep the information on your yard sign minimal: Your branding and name should stick out the most. If you add too much detail, the yard sign looks cluttered. No one can read your 24-word campaign slogan in inch-high letters on a yard sign. No one wants to.

Figure 12-1 lists good and bad examples of yard signs.

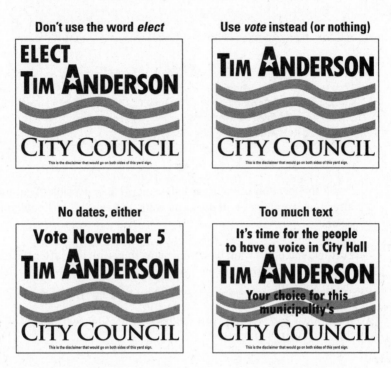

FIGURE 12-1:
Yard signs, good and bad.

Here's a summary:

Avoid putting the election date on a yard sign. If you win, or if you lose and want to run again, you can re-use the same yard sign, but only if it doesn't have a date on it.

Use the word *Vote* on the sign instead of *Elect*. If you win, you can reuse a yard sign with the word *Vote* on it; otherwise, you must fix *Elect* to say *Re-elect*. Or, you can avoid both terms; it's a campaign sign, and people aren't *that* slow.

Print the yard sign on both sides. Yes, it's cheaper to use just one side. Good yard sign placement mandates that the sign be visible to both lanes of traffic.

Placement

It helps to have some hardy volunteers plant your yard signs. Yes, you'll do your share of yard sign duty; keep signs in your car and at the ready. Also include some tools to help you hammer and dig, because not every location has the best soil.

DOUBLE YOUR YARD SIGN VISIBILITY

It's possible to increase your yard sign visibility without overspending. The trick is to relocate the signs, especially during the last two weeks of the campaign.

Most people tune out yard signs they've already seen. They recognize the bouquet of yard signs at major intersections, which eventually blend into the landscaping. However, if you go out and move the yard signs (keeping them in allowed locations), passersby will notice something different. Effectively, you've re-exposed the same people to a "new" yard sign without spending more money.

Track the location of your yard signs as well as possible. You must collect them after the campaign — and you do want to keep them should you choose to run again.

Further, you don't want your yard signs lingering long after the campaign. You're the candidate, so these rogue yard signs are your responsibility. It's your name on them, after all.

Rules exist for planting yard signs. Ensure that you know the rules and have informed your volunteers.

Writing letters to the editor

A great way to garner free advertising in the local paper is to get supporters to write letters to the editor. Some folks may do so without your prompting, but it helps to have a letter-writing campaign ready, because it's great exposure.

You can draft the letters yourself, which isn't unethical or wrong. Writing a good letter to the editor can be frustrating. You provide examples and have supporters sign and submit them. Trust me: Everyone does so.

Keep in mind the length on a good letter to the editor. Many publications limit the letters to 250 words or fewer. You want the letter to get to the point quickly and then mention your name. Short letters are best.

>> Remind the letter writers not to mention the competition, though, because anyone can write a letter, and someone will doubtless do so.

>> The best letters are admiration letters, especially from well-known citizens or individuals with a recognized name and reputation.

» Newspaper editors may enforce limitations on campaign letters. For example, they may publish only one campaign letter per person per election or limit submissions so that a single candidate doesn't dominate the editorial page. Contact the paper's editor to clarify any of these policies.

» Letters to the editor also provide an opportunity for someone other than yourself to rebut any attacks from your opposition.

Going door-to-door

Door-knocking is a time-honored political tradition and mandatory for first-time candidates. It's a good opportunity to meet people, but it also underscores some of the highs and lows you experience during a campaign; not everyone who opens their door is a supporter.

If you've never gone door-to-door, it can be intimidating. I know that when I've done it, I've felt like I'm intruding on people's privacy. Yet it is part of a valid campaign strategy and is the most personal way to connect with the voter.

When you approach a home, check for no-soliciting signs. Some campaign advisors say that you can ignore these signs because you're not truly a solicitor. I avoid these homes because I don't need to give anyone a reason not to vote for me. Make your own call.

Also pay attention to homes with signs about sleeping babies and people who work nights and sleep during the day. If the yard has a fence and a gate, you might want to think twice about entering.

Give the person a few moments to answer the door. Some people, especially the elderly, may not come to the door even though you see them inside. Respect their choice: Leave your literature and move on.

When you greet the voter, be polite. Introduce yourself and the office you seek. Hand them your rack card or other material. After giving your introduction, say something like, "I hope I can have your support." And because your material has your phone and email address, you can remind them to contact you if they have any questions. Most people will be happy at that point, and you can move on to the next house.

Try not to get too wound up in any conversation. Your goal is to complete a given number of houses or streets on your door-knocking route. Further, some people may seek to delay you on purpose. If so, smile and indicate that you must be moving on.

TIP

If someone indicates that they've already voted, thank them for doing so. If they voted for you, they'll tell you. Otherwise, they won't say whom they voted for. Do not ask them! Just move on.

Also, don't take it too hard if someone comes out and announces that they support your opponent. Sometimes you can tell so by seeing an opponent's yard sign on their lawn. If so, move on. Don't let the one voter disappoint you. Keep in mind the several other voters you connected with, and let those encounters brighten your day.

>> The best time to go door-to-door is when people are home — evenings and weekends. I don't door-knock after dark.

>> Incumbents need not go door-knocking. Still, some do, especially in a tight race.

>> Never assume that 1,000 doors equates to 1,000 voters. Your presence may make an impact, but keep in mind that informed voters use lots of data to make their decisions.

>> Refer to Chapter 7 for directions on preparing a walking list. You want to ensure that the doors you knock on have voters behind them.

Attending forums and debates

Candidate forums and debates aren't the drama you see in the movies. In fact, holding such forums isn't as common as you might think. Most of these events are rather dreary, attended by people who've already made up their minds and lacking in any gotcha moments or campaign-ending events.

The typical forum involves candidates seated at a table or on a dais. These are all candidates for a specific seat, district, or ward. Each candidate is given time for an introduction. Questions are asked of each candidate, usually the same question over and over, and candidates are provided time for a response. All candidates consume the full time allotted.

What are often labeled debates for a local election are forums again, though they might provide an opportunity for candidates to respond to each other. Rarely does a local election rise to the level of the historic Lincoln–Douglass debates.

Most of the reason that candidate forms lack gravity at the local level is that the issues are mundane. Yes, everyone loves the city. Yes, everyone supports the schools. Only a few minor issues separate the candidates. The key factor an informed voter looks for is who can think well on their feet. They want to vote for people who are likable. They're on the lookout for someone to screw up, lose their temper, or freeze at a key moment.

Rules for debates and forums

The number-one rule for any candidate forum or debate is to show up. Don't make a show of the event by saying that the hosting group is biased and therefore you won't attend. Don't fabricate an excuse that you're unavailable. Always show up to all events to which all candidates are invited.

Even if you're not invited, show up anyway! A local group may host their favorite candidate but fail to invite you. If the meeting is open to the public, show up. You need not cause a scene or do anything, but your presence will be noted.

A basic debate strategy

Before the event, determine how many candidates will share the stage with you. If the number is high, your answers will most likely match other candidates, so your goal is to stand out. Here are some suggestions:

>> Be concise. Answer a yes-no question with "yes" or "no" and stop talking. If the moderator opens the door for a longer response, make one.

>> Everyone loves to talk, but humans listen to only the first ten seconds or so of what you have to say. Make that part of your response the best. If you can't get your message out in ten seconds, practice.

>> Try not to take the full time to respond. It's tough to shut up, but you can learn.

>> Avoid getting into details. Numbers and specifics can trip you up. Speak in generalities. If the moderator asks for more information, direct them to your literature or website.

>> Smile. Look like you're enjoying yourself. In performance, the term is "to sell it." Look like you're doing the one thing everyone in the world would want to do at that time and like you're having a great time doing it.

Big problems in debates

In a candidate forum or debate, experienced politicians have an advantage: They've done it before. They know what works. You can learn as well, but you must have studied various forums and debates locally to understand how to apply yourself well.

A common trick an incumbent pulls is when a challenger makes an accusation. The incumbent replies, "Why haven't you contacted me in the past to bring up this issue?" This reply is an instant shutdown to whatever concern was raised. It shows that the challenger is making a hollow accusation.

Bone up on logical fallacies — for example, the strawman attack, bandwagon technique, and begging the question. The web has many sites that can train you in identifying these tactics, used mostly by amateurs, but that can be effectively shut down when you recognize them.

Don't forget to thank the hosts, especially if you're called on first either at the start of the forum or for the closing comments. After one candidate thanks the host, you don't need to repeat the thank-you.

At the closing, direct people to your website or social media accounts.

Writing press releases

Your campaign must generate at least one press release, to announce your candidacy. Other press releases may come, such as announcing events, developing new policies, and dealing with unforeseen events. The press most likely will cover your announcement, but you have no guarantee that they'll address anything further.

>> Update your media mailing list (refer to Chapter 9) to note how various reporters prefer to receive press releases: by snail mail, email, PDF, phone call, Twitter, and so on.

>> Also update your media mailing list with the reporter's deadlines or when they prefer to receive a story.

>> See Chapter 13 for additional press release suggestions.

Write the release

Ideally, the press release should fit on a single page, double-spaced. Print it on paper or electronically and use your campaign's letterhead.

Date the release. You can note whether it's for immediate release or to be held for a specific date or event. Even so, don't count on anything you give to the press being held to the date; if the story is worthy, they'll generate it immediately.

Start with a punchy headline. It should be strong and to the point, like a headline in a newspaper. In fact, many smaller newspapers and newsletters may print your press release as is.

Have a strong lead paragraph. Get the entire point across, putting as much information in the sentences as you can: the relevant date, your name, the issue, and so on. Use active verbs. Keep sentences short.

Check your facts. If you know a specific value and have a reference to back it up, use it. Otherwise, speak in general terms. Avoid exaggeration. For example, say "Too much has been spent" instead of "They've spent hundreds of thousands of dollars."

Don't forget your contact info, which should be part of the letterhead.

Proof the release. Beyond running it through the spell-checker, have someone else read it. Read it yourself aloud. Take a break before you send, and then read it again.

Press releases to consider

Beyond the initial press release announcing your candidacy, generate press releases as you campaign progresses.

Generate a press release for each endorsement you receive. Most endorsements come with a letter, which you can quote in your press release.

A press release can also comment on any news event affecting your office. If the government agency does something you object to, send out a press release.

COMMUNICATION METHODS TO CAREFULLY CONSIDER

The number of ways to connect with your audience is endless, especially with ever exploding technology and the ubiquity of mobile devices. For the methods listed here, I urge caution. You don't want to annoy or anger the voter.

Robocalls: I am not a fan of robocalls. Even if you get some bigwig to record it, people just can't abide hearing a robot on the line. It's not you or your campaign, it's abuse of the system by telemarketers and others. Avoid robocalls.

Group text messages: I consider a campaign text message to be spam. Receiving one, even from someone I support, is unpleasant. If possible, ensure that your supporters volunteer to receive a text message. Provide an easy way for them to opt out and remind them frequently that they can opt out.

Emails: Emails aren't as offensive as text messages, but keep in mind the same rules: Ensure that your supporters opt in on an email list. End your message with the instructions for unsubscribing. Remind them that you will never sell the list, though I recommend keeping the list for use should you become elected.

Tips and suggestions

Write about yourself in the third person. It may seem awkward, but everyone does it. If you want to say something in the press release, put it in quotes. Inside the quotes you can use *I* and *me* when referring to yourself.

Do not use a press release to attack your opponent. No newspaper or even a neighborhood flier will use a press release that contains a personal attack. If that's what you feel you need to do to get into office, perhaps you should rethink your goals.

To Go Negative

The negative campaign seems to be an American tradition, but what does negative campaigning really mean? You hear the terms *attack ads* and *mudslinging*. Often, they apply to anything critical.

Most negative campaign material is based in fact. It's only that the target doesn't like the facts pointed out that makes things seem "negative." And, of course, getting personal or fabricating mischief is also considered going negative, but in a vicious way. You must ask yourself if you need to do so to win and how effective such a strategy will be.

My advice is to run for local office on your own merits. Stay positive by showcasing your strengths and positions. This posture doesn't prevent your opponent from going negative on you, though, which is why you should know the turf even if you don't plan on trotting over it.

Understanding "going negative?"

You (the challenger) can be accused of going negative if you point out a disgruntled incumbent's dismal public record. In this case, the information is fair game. Like anything subjective, however, a spectrum exists for anything labeled an attack.

On the fair-criticism side of the spectrum, any elected official's public record, well-documented, is fair game. "My opponent has consistently voted for every property tax increase." Such a statement isn't an attack, though your opponent may think so.

The unfair side of the spectrum includes inuendo and outright slander. For example, bringing up an old public drunkenness charge is fair, but you must consider how it will play. Does the voter already know? How old is the charge? Better: Are you guilty of the same — or worse — sin?

IT'S OKAY TO SLANDER, KIND OF

As a candidate for office, you're considered a public person. As such, slander against you isn't actionable in court. People can and will say anything about you. If you threaten to sue, you show the voting public that your skin is far too thin to handle an elected position.

People have the right to criticize and to even make up stuff about public officials. What people don't have a right to do is maliciously attack them: Malicious slander is actionable in court. The problem, however, is to determine what is malicious. Typically, your slanderer must demonstrate a pattern of animosity toward you.

The good news is that truly slanderous, not to mention maliciously slanderous, attacks are rare in local elections. They show desperation and are a turnoff for many voters.

Going negative can also backfire. In a recent local race, a challenger criticized the incumbent for missing too many meetings. It turns out the incumbent was quite ill and spent weeks convalescing. In this example, the attack generated sympathy for the incumbent and derision toward the challenger, who eventually apologized. Not good.

>> Never attack your opponent personally.

>> Pointing out a fact isn't mudslinging, though you may be accused of it. Mudslinging itself is a series of unjust insults designed to damage an opponent's reputation. If someone accuses you of mudslinging, it's acceptable for you to clarify your statements as free from mudslinging.

Accepting that some people don't like you

Running for office introduces you to a new class of people: those you don't know who don't like you. It's amazing, but suddenly, and only because you dared run against someone they like, people will come out opposed to you and dream up all sorts of reasons to dislike you. This fact you must accept.

> *"Friends may come and go, but enemies accumulate"* —
> *Anonymous*

As a candidate, you may find yourself reintroduced to people you've wronged in the past. Maybe you've forgotten the incident. They haven't. Be prepared for them to make noise about it. (Refer to Chapter 4 to help you explore your past.)

THE UNDERVOTE

No one wins an election with 100 percent of the vote. Even when a candidate is fortunate enough to win unopposed, a phenomenon exists called the *undervote*. It's a meaningless statistic, but it's used by detractors to demonstrate that even an unopposed candidate isn't completely popular.

An undervote is calculated based on a comparison of the total votes in a contested election versus an uncontested election. For example, for seat A, the total number of votes for both candidates was 4,500. In seat B, where the incumbent ran unopposed, the total number of votes was 4,000. The difference shows an undervote of 500, meaning of all the people interested in seat A, 500 didn't give a rip about seat B.

Whether the undervote is due to people disliking an unopposed candidate is moot; the race was won regardless. Still, detractors and boo-birds love to point out undervoting as meaning something when it doesn't.

Some people, however, may dislike you for no rational reason. You may find them popping up like weeds on social media or in the paper. Don't bother trying to understand why they dislike you. Merely accept it and move on. These people aren't voting for you anyway. Trying to change their minds is a waste of time.

Unleashing your wrath

One campaign tactic is to hit your opponent with a negative or attack piece during the last week of the election. This strategy provides little time for the opponent to respond, though with the Internet and social media, the capability to address a last-minute attack is stronger than ever.

If you decide to unleash your wrath, do it as positively as possible. One tactic is to list two columns, one for you and one for your opponent. You compare and contrast policy differences between you, which is fair and not negative (though it's selective). Figure 12-2 shows an example.

Going full-on negative probably isn't necessary. It may be seen as a sign of desperation, especially if the attacks are personal or flat-out incorrect. It's best to stay on point unless the entire campaign has been a giant mudfest, in which case the voters are disgusted anyhow.

>> Going negative is easy, which is why so many candidates do it.

>> Negative attacks work both ways: they attack your opponent, but they also reflect upon you. It's easy to lose support if you suddenly go negative.

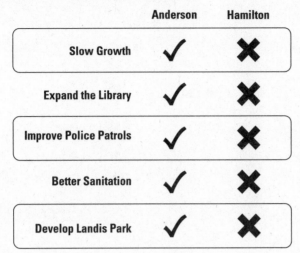

Know The Difference This November!

	Anderson	Hamilton
Slow Growth	✓	✗
Expand the Library	✓	✗
Improve Police Patrols	✓	✗
Better Sanitation	✓	✗
Develop Landis Park	✓	✗

FIGURE 12-2:
An "attack" comparison piece.

>> The consequence of criticizing someone is that they'll naturally become defensive and deny or justify their behavior. Don't let this happen to you! The defense doesn't play the game to score a touchdown.

>> The voters remember a negative campaign. It builds resentment that doesn't disappear, even if you should win.

Preparing your defense

You've been attacked. Your opponent or one of their supporters has decided to take the campaign to a nasty level. They accuse you of starting it, of course, but offer no proof. You're left determining how best to defend yourself or whether it's even necessary.

If you've performed a SWOT analysis on yourself (refer to Chapter 6), you may be able to guess what's coming. If so, you've prepared a defense and are ready with a press release or another way to address the issue. Being prepared is truly the best way to deal with a legitimate issue.

Don't waste time worrying about a false accusation. Sure, anyone can make up anything and hurl it your way. Odds are good, however, that no one will fabricate something against you. You may catch wind of something from the rumor mill. If so, and if the accusation isn't true, it's a ruse designed to divert your attention. Ignore it.

If need be, meet with your campaign team and discuss how best to deal with potential problems. You may find that voters in local elections have a strong distaste for nasty politics. The problem may resolve itself.

IN THIS CHAPTER

» **Working for your campaign**

» **Setting priorities**

» **Engaging volunteers**

» **Contacting early voters**

» **Getting out your message**

» **Dealing with screw-ups**

» **Staying positive until the end**

Chapter **13**

The Campaign

With all the pieces in place — material generated, volunteers coordinated, and funds incoming — you're ready for the campaign. The days count down swiftly to the election.

Though you've been organizing and working for weeks, the official start of the campaign is at the end of the filing period. Minor deadlines fill the time between the filing period and election day, with the campaign gaining urgency and momentum as it progresses. The experience will be like nothing you've done before.

REMEMBER

DAN SAYS

» You volunteered to run for office.

» The key to implementing any campaign strategy is funding. Your monetary resources determine the campaign's scope. Refer to Chapter 11.

» Have fun. I try to make all my campaigns fun to keep the volunteers and supporters cheerful and engaged. Even when I know I'll lose, I stay positive and on-message. That's the best strategy of all.

Your Campaign's Number-One Employee

For the duration of the campaign, you must be dedicated to the cause. You will do most, if not all, of the work. Consider your campaign advisors and volunteers as support people. They are not your employees; the candidate (you) is the only employee. And no, you're not getting paid.

Taking on a full-time job

Once the filing period ends, you know who your opponents are and how many are in the field. Only then does your campaign strategy solidify and you become aware of the specific tasks necessary to win.

You can get quite a bit done for the campaign before the end of the filing period: initial fundraising, gathering volunteers, establishing a brand, setting your message, getting material printed, and so on. These tasks are mild compared to the demands on your schedule *after* the filing period.

The weeks preceding the election will be some of the busiest you've ever experienced. Being a candidate is time-consuming, and eventually it will eclipse your full-time job and other duties you've assumed — especially in an active, highly contested race.

During the campaign, you will experience emotional highs and lows. It will be stressful. In fact, it's my observation that, come the weekend before election day, all candidates gladly welcome knowing that the ordeal will soon be over.

>> Dedicate yourself to the campaign. Make yourself available. The demands build as the campaign progresses, but be aware of these demands early so that they don't creep up on you later.

>> Quite a few candidates, including incumbents, wait until the last minute to file.

Clearing your calendar

If you haven't done so already, review your schedule during the campaign. As the candidate, you must remain flexible. Forums and fundraisers can pop up at the last minute. Dates will change. You must take advantage of opportunities, because your opponents certainly will.

CAMPAIGN CALENDAR

» Use your campaign calendar to keep track of events, but also compare it with your regular calendar to avoid conflicts.

» Never say, "Oh, I'm busy that day," "My kid's recital is that weekend," or "I'm out of town on business." You might get away with these excuses in the first few weeks of the campaign, but as the campaign progresses — whether your excuse is legitimate or not — backing out of an event comes across as dubious.

» Even established dates in a campaign may change. The big forum put on by the Business Luncheon Club may change to a different week. Be flexible.

» Your schedule will become busier as the campaign progresses.

Making those calls

As the campaign's full-time and only employee (who isn't being paid), it's your job to be on the phone setting appointments, contacting supporters, and raising funds.

Yes, few people enjoy making calls, organizing, and especially asking for donations. If you have an enthusiastic supporter, put them in charge of volunteers. Still, as the candidate, your job is to make the important calls.

» Set aside a given time during the day to call for donations. Try to make the calls when you know people are available.

» Also see Chapter 11 for hints and suggestions on fundraising and other money stuff.

Putting your volunteers to work

Hopefully, you have a rich harvest of volunteers, eager to help you. Don't neglect them! Per the directions in Chapter 9, create a list of your volunteers and contact them to assign various jobs and duties during the campaign.

Here are some jobs and duties you should consider assigning to your volunteer army:

Yard sign managers: These volunteers help plant and move yard signs. Have a chief yard sign manager help you keep track of where the signs are planted, and police the yard signs that have been damaged, kicked, and unceremoniously removed.

Social media fans: For a local-office election, you should be the one generating tweets and social media postings. Still, you can enlist your volunteers to like, share, and comment on the posts.

Door-knockers: You should do most of the door-knocking, but having an army to walk with you allows you to complete your door quota: Assign volunteers to different streets so that you cover a larger area quickly. Even if they're not up to door-knocking, engage volunteers to organize maps for where to go.

Data crunchers: If you know computer people, have them help you with your lists. For non-computer people, assign volunteers to gather phone numbers and email contacts. This process can happen when you go door-to-door or afterward to help organize and maintain the lists.

Fundraiser hosts and guests: Volunteers can not only host a fundraiser for you but can also attend other fundraisers. At the fundraiser, your volunteers can interact with others, share their enthusiasm for your campaign, and answer questions.

Envelope stuffers: It's amazing how many envelopes you can stuff, address, and stamp in an hour when you have a room full of eager volunteers. Even two or three people make the time go faster.

Get-out-the-vote volunteers: You need volunteers to make last-minute phone calls to ensure that all known supporters have already voted or are heading to the polls. If not, have volunteers pick up people and drive them to the polls.

Sounding boards: Don't forget your volunteers when it comes time to run a new idea, to proofread, or just to obtain moral support.

If your volunteers don't do these jobs, you get the honor. Otherwise, you can be their volunteer leader. Call your volunteers frequently to see how they're doing. Ask them whether they need anything from you, such as yard signs or handouts. Remind them of how important they are to you and the campaign.

Above all, don't forget to thank your volunteers.

REMEMBER

Not One, but Two Elections

The modern political contest is two elections rolled into one: the absentee election and the contest on election day. Your campaign must devise a strategy for both. And, if you're running for a partisan position, you must do so twice again — once in the primary and again in the general election.

Running in the primary and general elections

For those local offices that are partisan, you find yourself in two elections. The first is the *primary*, when candidates run to represent their party. The second election is the *general* election, where the primary winners — along with any independents — vie to win the seat.

For these races, you double your efforts. You must craft a campaign for the primary, including efforts to reach absentee voters as well as those voting on the primary date. This struggle is repeated in the fall for the general election, with a new set of opponents.

>> In districts where one party dominates, the primary election is effectively the general election. Due to people voting the party line, if you win the dominant party's nod, you're pretty much a shoo-in for the general election. Still, never take anything for granted.

>> Winning a primary means you may win party support for the general election. This support could mean donations, advertising, volunteers, and other benefits. It's not a guarantee, however: Some parties may prefer to focus on statewide and national races as opposed to local ones.

>> A trend in some states is to put the top two vote-getters from the primary on the general election ballot, even if both are from the same party. In this type of election, party support may be lacking as the general election merely becomes a primary in which every voter casts a ballot.

Addressing the absentees

The first crop of voters cast their ballots in the absentee election. Yes, it's the same election with the same election day, but these folks vote early. You must reach them before they vote for someone else.

The best way to approach absentee voters is to send them introductory material. Using your list of predictable absentee voters (refer to Chapter 7), prepare a mailer. It can be a letter or a card.

When absentee ballots are mailed to early voters, send them a *chaser* card. This material targets the early voter specifically. You want the chaser to arrive before or on the day the voter receives their early ballot. It would be the second reminder for them to consider voting for you.

As more early ballots are sent out, send out chasers to those voters. You obtain the list from the election authority. It's a public record, though you may have to pay to obtain a copy. Take the addresses and use them to send out your chasers.

If you can afford it, always send out chasers by first-class mail. You can use a postcard stamp if the chaser qualifies as a postcard. Only in a huge election with a lot of voters should you consider using a bulk mailing house for absentee chasers. At the bulk rate, you may not be assured that your material will arrive in time.

REMEMBER

CAMPAIGN CALENDAR

DAN SAYS

>> Absentee voting can start as early as a few weeks after the filing period ends.

>> The agency running the election may have a posted date when it sends out ballots to early voters. This date is the deadline you use for sending out your introductory letter. Ensure that it arrives as close as possible to the date on which people receive their ballots.

>> A good tactic to use for your introductory mailer is to send an absentee ballot application with your material — if such a thing is permissible by the election authority in your state. Urge the voter to fill it out if they haven't already.

>> I've heard some campaign advisors claim that early voters mark their ballots within three days of receiving them. Whether the timeframe is that quick or longer, the point is to be timely with the chasers. No one can take back a vote after they've mailed in their ballot.

Working the general election

Your goal for the general election is to connect with as many voters as possible. An effective way to do so is with campaign mailers. The ideal quantity is three, though few local campaigns generate enough revenue to send out three mailers.

If you can afford it, send the three mailers to your list of chronic voters. If not, you can target specific neighborhoods, precincts, or wards. Use your analysis of voter data (refer to Chapter 7) to determine which areas of the district have the biggest turnout or where voters might be inclined to support you. Target those areas with specific mailers.

The timing of your material is vital. You want the three mailers to go out late in the campaign. If it's too early, the voter will forget you sent anything. Too late and your material may arrive after the election. Sending out the three pieces in the final two weeks of the election works best.

All three pieces should be positive, reminding the voter of who you are and why you're running. Remember to add any endorsements you've received.

Some campaign managers tend to urge a negative piece to attack your opponent late in the campaign. Though this technique is fun, it carries the risk of backfiring, especially if the material consists of a personal attack. A comparison piece on the issues is a better approach. Refer to Chapter 12 for more information on going negative.

Door-knocking also helps you to connect with voters for the general election. It's not as efficient, however, as a mailer. Because going door-to-door takes so much time, the operation must start early. The further from the election you door-knock, the more likely voters are to forget that you stopped by.

REMEMBER

>> Refer to Chapter 12 for additional ways to connect with the voter during the campaign.

>> If you're running in a partisan election, enlist help from your local party to get out your message and provide other support for the general election.

>> Don't forget newspaper advertising. It may not have the same reach as direct mail, but it's easy to put together when time and money are tight. Radio is also inexpensive, though with both the newspaper and radio, ensure that the audience is large enough to justify the expense.

>> Bulk mail for your final pieces is okay, but first-class postage reaches the voter on time. If you like, use bulk to send out pieces the week before the election, and then send out the final piece first-class.

OH, NO! IT'S A RUNOFF!

Some states feature runoff elections when a single candidate fails to garner more than 50 percent of the vote. If this rule holds in your election and you're one of the two top vote-getters, the election isn't over: It's sudden-death overtime.

The rules for runoff elections vary. Generally, the period is short, only a few weeks. The second election day comes quickly. The good news is that both candidates face the same restriction. The bad news is that you may have to refocus your campaign material and inject some enthusiasm into yourself and your weary volunteers.

If you received the most votes in the general election, the odds favor you to win the runoff election. I don't know any specific example of the second-place candidate ever winning a runoff. Because of this foregone conclusion, many localities are eschewing the runoff election and granting the win to whichever candidate won the plurality in the general election.

Stuff Happens

In preparing for battle, I have always found that plans are useless, but planning is indispensable. —Dwight D. Eisenhower

No matter how well you laid out your campaign strategy, things happen that disturb the flow. For example, your opponent may drop out of the race. That would be a good, and highly unlikely, thing. More common, however, are issues that come to light late, which you must be prepared to act upon.

>> The issues can be positive or negative. For example, your opponent may have committed a major gaffe and it's receiving play in the press and online. On the other hand, a speeding ticket you just received may have been innocent several months back, but now it becomes a campaign issue for your opponent.

>> The key to dealing with interesting stuff that occurs during the campaign is to remain flexible with your funding. Is the money not coming in? Get on the phone and raise more!

Enduring a major screw-up

You must own up to any mistakes you make during the campaign. It's important that you do so as close to the event as possible. Blaming staff or an underling is extremely bad form; accept responsibility yourself, even if you weren't directly involved.

When your opponent screws up, gauge the public's response. Most likely, you can safely stay above the fray. Amateur politicians are good at mishandling errors in judgment and demonstrating questionable behavior. If your opponent is shooting himself in the foot, stand back and smile.

>> Owning up to a major screw-up won't change the minds of people who already oppose you. They'll parade your blunder up and down the street, beating drums and chanting loudly. Who cares?

>> Hopefully, you've reviewed your background enough to ensure that any skeletons in your closet won't come out. Refer to Chapter 4.

>> False accusations against you underscore your opponent's desperation.

>> Don't blame your opponent for an attack when it comes from one of their supporters. Dismiss the attack as gossip or inuendo irrelevant to the campaign.

DAN SAYS

» Do not engage with trolls online.

» Your goal is to be a statesman, which is a high compliment for a politician. Whether handling an error on your part or avoiding getting into a fracas over your opponent's error, demonstrate a calm and reasonable response.

» It's amazing how many things you think are major screw-ups turn out to be nothing. Prepare a response to a major screw-up, but don't deliver it unless you're called upon. After all, if no one notices, you can let it slide and move on.

Dealing with a family emergency

Everyone respects the importance of family. The public knows that you give up a lot of your private life during a campaign. If you have a family emergency and cannot campaign, write a press release, post on social media, and let your supporters know as much as you're comfortable telling them. The public will understand.

» If something comes up that requires your attention to a degree greater than the campaign allows, take the time off.

» Alas, the family emergency is often abused by candidates who just want to hide out. Don't let candidates who fabricate a crisis dissuade you from taking a legitimate break from a campaign when a true emergency arises.

Down to the Wire

Close to election day, you arrive at a point when you can campaign no more. You're exhausted. All the planning is complete. Momentum pushes you toward election day. You'll be glad it's going to be over soon.

Even when you smell impending doom, remain positive. Never let your gut feelings alter your attitude in public. People will remember that you held up well and they'll be willing to support you again. Contrast this attitude with the sour grapes candidate who blames staff or the public. No voter wants to see someone like that again.

Chapter **14**

Election Day

A ll your campaign's energy is focused on election day, getting the individual in the voting booth to help thrust you into the waiting embrace of a government office. You have several options to keep your day busy, but most of the campaigning is done. After you vote, you wait for the polls to close. Then you suffer through the anxiety of waiting for the first results to be posted. It will be a day unlike any other.

» Initial results are posted about an hour after the polls close, and sometimes longer. Generally, the counting is over by midnight, though the timing depends on voter turnout.

» In some states with mail-in voting, the final tally may not be official for some time after election day.

DAN SAYS

» Don't plan on doing anything the day after the election. Yes, it's a workday, the Wednesday that follows Tuesday. (And I'm still puzzled why elections are held on Tuesdays.) You'll most likely be up late, so keep Wednesday clear for whatever happens next.

Get Out the Vote

The last phase of a campaign, starting the weekend before the election and even taking place on election day, is your get-out-the-vote effort. You want to ensure that all your supporters know about election day and make it to the polls to cast their ballots in your favor.

Never assume that everyone is going to vote. It may have been your priority for weeks, but for the average citizen, it's just another Tuesday. I'm serious: You must make efforts to ensure that your supporters make it to the polls. Here are some ideas:

Organize phone trees. Have your volunteers contact supporters. These phone numbers should have been gathered when you went door-to-door. Make the call. Remind them to vote.

Drive people to the polls. If people find it inconvenient to get out and vote, offer to drive them. Line up volunteers who can assist people to their polling places.

Wave signs. Arrange for volunteers to stand at busy intersections or outside polling places and wave your signs. This activity increases awareness of the election and provides another name imprint in your favor.

These efforts should pay off, especially in a close election. What you don't want to hear on Wednesday is someone saying they couldn't make it to the polls after you lost by only a couple of votes.

» Get-out-the-vote is abbreviated GOTV. It's not a television station.

» I'm not a fan of sign-waving, because it seems like a silly waste of time. Still, on election day, you have nothing else do to.

» When you sign-wave, most people who drive by will ignore you. You'll get some honks and thumbs-up from supporters. Detractors may shout nasty things or flash the finger. Just smile and wave.

Rules About Election Day

The voting booth is private. That you voted is a public record; whom you vote for is recorded only as a vote for that person, not a vote by you. The government is serious about this sanctity. The rules covering it fall under the category of electioneering.

Electioneering itself is another term for campaign activities. The electioneering laws, however, prohibit those activities within or around a polling place: You cannot campaign, solicit votes, hand out material, hold a yard sign, or otherwise influence a voter within a given distance from the polling location or people standing in line to vote.

Details about electioneering on election day, as well as other restrictions, vary from state to state. Your candidate packet should list these rules; otherwise, you must contact the election authority and they'll provide a review.

Fines and other punishments are applied to those who break these rules. Enforcement varies, as is the case everywhere. But as a good candidate, be mindful not to unduly influence voters on election day.

>> Electioneering laws may also apply to locations that accept early, in-person, or walk-in voting.

>> When you vote, you can still wear a campaign button or T-shirt. Specific rules on this attire vary from state to state, but if the button isn't obnoxiously large, it's okay.

>> If the poll workers notify you or a volunteer of violating electioneering laws, be respectful and cease at once.

POLL WATCHING

Some political types make hay regarding the topic of poll-watching. Because elections are set by state or local rules, what constitutes poll-watching can vary.

In most cases, poll watchers are people officially designated by the election authority to observe interactions at a polling place. They can be party officials or represent an issue or a candidate on the ballot. Their purpose is to help ensure the integrity of the election; poll watchers are not poll workers.

Many rules or restrictions surround the topic of poll-watching. The election authority has any information you may need, should you designate poll watchers. The candidate cannot be a poll watcher.

Plan Your Victory Party

One question you'll be asked during the closing weeks of the campaign is the location of your victory party. Or, it should just be a "party" that you hope turns into a victory party. It may be something you plan specifically, though most likely it will be a collective effort put together by volunteers or other, like-minded candidates.

You can start your victory party efforts by asking around to see which other candidates have scheduled such an event. Often, the local political parties put on events, to which they invite candidates in a nonpartisan election who may lean one way or the other.

When no one has set up a victory party, do it yourself. Find a restaurant or bar willing to serve as a venue. You don't need to reserve a room; any location that can accommodate a few dozen people works. Remember: Elections are held on a Tuesday. Any restaurant or bar will welcome the business.

If possible, ensure that a TV is available where you can view the results. Having a computer available is also a must, because you want to see the tallies as they're posted on the election website. You'll be hitting the Refresh key often as the results come in.

During the event, ensure that you stop by and thank your supporters. Make an extra effort to express appreciation for your volunteers. Name them. Thank them in front of the group.

You can prepare an acceptance or concession speech, though I've never done so. You should, however, have something ready to say to the press should they attend or phone.

For a local election, it's not necessary to make a concession phone call to the victor. The race results speak for themselves.

REMEMBER

>> The Refresh key for most web browsers is Ctrl+R, Command+R on the Mac.

>> The press will want to know the victory party's location. If not, they'll want to know when you're available so that they can get a quote.

>> Thank the voters. Remember, our system may not pick the best candidate, but you accept the results.

The Aftermath

It's over. You experience the elation of victory or the icy numbness of defeat. You can run a flawless campaign, do everything right, and still lose an election. Or, you can be certain of defeat, only to be surprised by a last-minute victory. The voters have the final word.

» The first immediate task you must undertake, win or lose, is to clean up your yard signs. You can direct your volunteers to do so, though ultimately it's your responsibility to remove the signs.

» Post a thank-you to the voters on social media and your website. If the campaign can afford it, run a thank-you advertisement in the local paper.

Accepting a loss

It's okay to be disappointed after losing an election. It's not okay to be bitter and public with your anger. No matter what the turnout, people voted for you. Don't disappoint them.

Avoid making any long-term predictions after a loss, specifically about your political future. You may be asked about another run. Answer vaguely. It's difficult to make a clear decision when you've just wobbled off the emotional rollercoaster.

Above all, give yourself time. Wait a few days before you do any serious reflection or analysis of the results. All candidates in an election help shape the debate. The effect you've had is far greater than your loss immediately leads you to believe.

» A first-time loss can be disappointing, but if the totals were close, take heart. Especially against an incumbent or well-known first-time contender, a close election shows that you have wide support and should consider running again.

» Review detailed voting data, when it's available, to see how you did. You may find that the race was quite close in a few districts, wards, or precincts. You might also discover that poor turnout in some areas also affected your race. This is good data to use should you choose to run again.

» It may be difficult to point to one specific factor that cost you the election. In most cases, however, it's a lack of name recognition.

>> Few outsiders make it into public office unless a resounding issue has drawn the voters' attention. Despite the chronic griping about state and national governments, and outside of major cities, most Americans are content with local government.

Dealing with a win

Winning anything is marvelous. An election is even more so because it's personal. People voted for *you*. Don't let this instant popularity go to your head, however; the public has a First Amendment right to criticize elected officials, and you're now one of them. The honeymoon is short.

On election night, ensure that you don't gloat or put down your opponent or "spike the football." Be professional and courteous.

The next day, you most likely will receive phone calls. Supporters will call, of course, but you'll also receive calls from the organization the public just hired you to join. You will be welcomed aboard.

The next few weeks will be busy as you attempt to get up to speed on various issues. Being elected is like catching a moving train. The business of government doesn't stop just because a new suit sits in one of the high-back chairs.

>> Yes, you'll receive a congratulatory call from people within government who might have been openly opposed to your campaign and aren't too pleased with your election. Don't let the calls surprise you.

>> Part 4 of this book covers the role of the elected official.

Agonizing over close elections

Ask any election official: They'll tell you the preferred results are when the winner is obvious. They like tallies where hundreds (or more) votes separate the candidates. Close elections are a nightmare for these people — as well as for the candidates and everyone else paying attention.

If your election is close, let the rules for automatic recounts work. Most election laws provide that if the race is within a certain percentage difference between two candidates, the ballots are run again. The system works. Accept the results.

What you don't want to do is demand a recount when the law doesn't automatically provide for one. First, your campaign must pay for the recount. Second, and most important, you come off as a sore loser. This antic reduces your chance of being taken seriously again as a candidate for public office.

>> Automatic recounts are paid for by the election authority or the district holding the election. Only when you request a recount must you pay for one.

>> Rarely does a recount yield results different from the original tally.

>> Ties in elections happen more often than you think, especially for local elections in small districts where only a dozen or so people vote. The rules for settling a tie vary, including the coin-toss method.

WARNING

>> Never sue because you believe the election was stolen. Sure, it might have been, but such a thing is nearly impossible to prove. Unless you have enough people confess to illegal voting or otherwise manipulating the ballot, a judge will never overturn an election.

Why Not Try Again?

You ran a positive campaign with a respectable showing. After the sting of defeat grows dull, consider running again. Your supporters will welcome your eagerness to press on.

A second try at the same office is why I recommend keeping your yard signs generic. (Refer to Chapter 12.) You can easily reuse yard signs in a subsequent election, as you can reuse your branding. Your messaging, however, must be updated to reflect the new race. Voter lists must also be refreshed and new strategies presented.

Before you next run, stay involved. If you didn't rock the boat too much, you may find yourself appointed to government committees. Otherwise, continue your role as an outspoken activist for better government. Don't give up.

>> You may not win the second time, but if you receive more votes in the next election, consider a third attempt. You want to see a positive trend in voting results: 42 percent and then 48 percent. This effect is the public getting to know and trust you. Run again.

>> If the voting percentage you receive in subsequent elections is flat or declines, don't consider another run. Refer to Chapter 3 for other ways you can effect change in your community.

THE PERENNIAL CANDIDATE

Two types of candidates fall into the *perennial* category: those who desperately want to be elected to anything and those who run as placeholders for the minority party.

Desperate perennial candidates are stubbornly persistent, running in race after race and trying to win any office. They run for city council, state legislature, sheriff, water board, and on and on. They may not show any improvement in their election results. Indeed, most are probably in the game for some attention.

Placeholders are the loyal opposition. Found more often in partisan races, they run to hold the minority party's place on the ballot, rarely campaign, and hope for the best. Yet, sometimes this persistence can pay off.

Both types of perennial candidates run terrible campaigns, one because they're desperate and the other because they know the odds. I trust you'll do better: Run a good campaign, focus on the issues, and keep at it. A persistent candidate stands a better chance than the typical one-and-done candidate.

In Office

4

Chapter **15**

Know the Law

Welcome to an elected position in local government. You are vested with certain powers, far fewer than you had otherwise believed. Further, you're shackled by laws, rules, and code that would be prohibitive on any private citizen. Such is the price you pay for taking on the role of elected official.

A key step to holding office is to know the law. Like a game of Monopoly but with real money (and real jail), rules govern your role. You have duties defined and powers granted. You may have a few months to study up on the rules, or you may find yourself taking office immediately. Either way, you must know the law.

Orientation

As a newly elected official, you're offered training to assist in taking on your new responsibilities and doing the job properly. This training may be provided by the agency you're joining or by a professional organization related to the government body. The training is usually a day long, and I urge you to attend.

Pay attention during the training. The people putting it on are experts and may know more than some within the government body you're joining. Now is the time to pepper them with questions.

For example, if the topic is conflicts of interest, ask a hypothetical question: "If my neighbor is applying for a conditional-use permit, must I recuse myself from deliberation?" Others present also benefit from the answer.

Keep whatever material and handouts are provided. The training can be overwhelming, so it's good to have material available so that you can refer to it later.

>> Incumbents who win reelection often attend elected-officials training to brush up on their roles as well as study new laws that affect their position.

>> The agency pays for your attendance at the training, which may also include meals, lodging, and transportation.

>> Training may not clue you in to certain ongoing issues within the organization itself. For that job, you rely on staff such as the clerk or attorney to brief you. A packet may also be provided.

>> Start attending meetings regularly after your election win. The organization may also supply you with an information packet so that you can read the material.

>> For another resource, take advantage of elected officials and their experience. Ask them for advice and input. They've been where you are and may have kind words of advice.

>> Then again, when I joined my first elected body, many of those already seated were not pleased with my victory. To say they were less than helpful would be an understatement.

TIP

REMEMBER

DAN
SAYS

Rules

Most of the perceived insanity of government is evident by its adherence to the rules that regulate its operation. Unlike an individual or a private business, a government agency is owned by the public. Therefore, it's the public's right to know what the agency does and, in the United States, to limit that agency's power to a defined role.

To keep any governing body inline, rules are set to determine what's allowed, what's forbidden, and the processes to undertake to accomplish the agency's various duties. Elected officials fall under these rules, which are written down in state, county, or local code.

DAN SAYS

>> People have rights. Government has powers.

>> Government powers are outlined specifically in the code.

>> Two schools of thought govern the breadth of a local agency's powers: home rule and Dillon's rule. A *home rule* agency's powers aren't limited to those enumerated in the code. Such an agency could take on a new task if it likes, creating its own powers for itself. A *Dillon's rule* agency can do only those tasks provided for in code. For example, if the code doesn't allow your city to start its own space program, it cannot do so. Your state constitution as well as existing legal decisions determine whether your agency operates under home rule or Dillon's rule.

Knowing the code

The rules governing your agency's duties as well as what you as an elected official can and cannot do should have been reviewed during your new-official training. (Refer to the earlier section "Orientation.") Ensure that you review these rules to become familiar with them. It's not your job to enforce them; that duty falls to staff. It is important, however, that you have a grasp on what the rules enforce.

Consider the code as the rules of the game. They tell you the goal, how to play, how to take turns, and what do when certain situations arise. Your role is to abide by the rules so that the decisions you make for the organization are aligned with the law and the agency's stated intent.

Here's an example of a common rule for government agencies:

1. The date and time of an agency meeting must be published a week in advance of the meeting.

2. The meeting's agenda must be published a week in advance of the meeting.

3. The meeting place must be accessible to the public.

4. No changes to the meeting date, time, place, or agenda can be made without an emergency declaration by the agency.

These rules make sense because the agency must be transparent and conduct the public's business in public. So when Commissioner Rose decides at the last minute that she wants to discuss redistricting during the meeting, but because her issue isn't on the agenda, it can't be brought up.

Staff assists you in following the rules. Unfortunately, staff cannot tell you what to do, which puts them in a tight spot. Therefore, it's up to the elected officials to know and adhere to the code as best they can.

If you have any doubt about what the rules are that govern your job in the agency, consult with the agency's attorney.

>> Like the rules of any game, adherence is up to the players. It's common for small agencies, generally lacking public oversight, to drift from their original intent. Experience shows that few elected officials get away with such disregard for the code.

>> Punishments are provided in code for violation of the rules. In most cases, any illegal actions taken are rendered void. For ethical violations, fines can be levied on the elected officials.

Visiting your paid expert

The legal quagmire of rules that govern a district as well as its elected officials is overwhelming. No one expects you to know everything, but no one wants you to be ignorant, either. The go-to person for any questions you have is the agency's attorney. Technically, the attorney's job is to provide you with legal advice as an elected official.

THE HIERARCHY OF LAWS

Government rules cascade from the top down, in a structure that parallels the political divisions of your state. At the top is the state constitution, which is the framework that describes how the state government is implemented and operates.

Below the state constitution are the statutes and codes that provide the functional details describing how the government is run. These statutes specifically address issues such as elections, taxes, and the operations of the agency you've joined.

At the local level, laws, codes, and ordinances are enacted to govern the agency's district. The scope of these rules is set by statute; many of them are required, with others created to resolve issues specific to the local agency.

Within the organization, policies determine issues not addressed elsewhere. These policies determine how the agency handles specific procedures, sets limits, and so on.

At some point early in your elected life, visit with the attorney. You don't need to have a question ready; lawyers do all the talking, regardless. Still, don't be shy about asking questions. If your agency's attorney doesn't have an immediate answer, expect one soon.

Especially on matters of ethics or questions regarding proper procedure, always check with the attorney. Even when other elected officials disagree with you, the attorney has an obligation to inform you of the law, regardless of what others think.

>> Attorneys can be wrong. You can disagree with them, but obtaining their opinion is part of the process. It shows that you made an effort to find information or remedy a situation.

>> The answers the attorney provides to your personal inquiry may be shared with the full board. The attorney represents you as a member of that board; therefore, the entire board is entitled to hear the answer.

>> The agency's attorney isn't your free personal attorney. They won't help you with personal legal issues or represent you in court for charges made against you as a private citizen.

>> When in doubt, always contact the agency attorney.

Conflicts of Interest

Affecting politicians at all levels of office are rules regarding conflicts of interest. This is the mine-laden ground upon which clumsy elected officials create the most noise and animosity regarding their decisions.

A *conflict of interest* occurs when your public decisions offer you or someone close to you a pecuniary benefit. The range of benefit is rather broad, which makes determining some conflicts of interest obvious but others difficult.

Fortunately, elected officials have been abusing the system to their own advantage long enough that plenty of rules and thoughts are available to peruse regarding real, potential, and imaginary conflicts of interest.

>> A *pecuniary* benefit is a financial one, though conflicts of interest may not be limited to monetary benefits.

>> For example, having your talentless niece cast as the lead in the school musical would be perhaps a type of benefit to a school board member.

Determining a conflict of interest

The general rule for a conflict of interest goes like this: If you think it's a conflict of interest, it is. Recuse yourself. This choice means you won't take part in any decision made on the issue, you won't vote, and, in many situations, you excuse yourself from the room.

Specifically, conflicts of interest are defined by statute. These statewide laws cover all elected officials, though the degree may change, depending on the district.

The bottom line with all conflict-of-interest rules is this: Will you or someone close to you personally benefit from your decision? The obvious example is awarding your company the new heavy-equipment contract. When you vote yes, and against a competing company, you're putting your personal interests ahead of the people's.

Above all, check with the agency's attorney if you suspect a potential conflict of interest. They offer advice on how to deal with the issue, though they can't specifically tell you what to do. And their advice is just that; it's not an order. If you don't feel a conflict is present, it's your decision to vote on the topic, but be aware of the political backlash you may face later.

>> Though voting for a tax cut can be considered a pecuniary benefit, it's not a conflict of interest. The conflict must be personal, directly beneficial to you or someone close to you. A tax cut affects everyone, so vote to cut all you want.

>> Conflicts of interest deal with degrees of separation between you and the individual with the conflict. Degree 0 is you. Degree 1 is an immediate family member. Two degrees indicate in-laws and other, less-close families. Conflict-of-interest laws classify these degrees, illustrating how close a conflict must be before action on your behalf is necessary.

>> Study the state's ethics laws as well as any local policies regarding conflicts of interest, to ensure that you understand all the issues.

>> If you recuse yourself from a decision, leave the room. It's a disappointment for me when I see an elected official declare a conflict yet remain on the dais or just push back their chair. If you've "conflicted out," stand up and walk out until the decision has been made.

Dealing with a conflict

Having a conflict of interest doesn't necessarily eliminate you from making a decision. In fact, for some low-population districts, conflicts of interest are inevitable. Everyone on the town council has had a job or a family member who has worked at the grocery store that's looking for a zone change. The government must make a decision, so you plow ahead. The key for dealing with the conflict is full disclosure.

At most public meetings, either before the entire meeting or before specific agenda items, the mayor or chairman asks, "Does anyone want to declare a conflict." That's your opportunity to let the sun shine on your connection.

For example, you can say, "Your honor, my brother-in-law works for one of the applicants, though I don't feel this conflict will affect my decision." Better would be, "Your honor, my brother-in-law works for one of the applicants. I've spoken with our attorney and he has advised me that this is not a conflict of interest."

Then again, keep in mind that perception is everything. Even with full disclosure, when in doubt, opt out.

>> Declaring a conflict need not excuse you from the decision. It's just that your decision will be tainted by the public who believes you have something to benefit.

>> People who oppose you will criticize your decision, in many cases regardless of what action you take.

HAVE SOME FREE LUNCH

Movers and shakers desire to get to know the people who hold public office. They may ask you out for coffee or lunch. Take the meeting. It's good for you, the organization, and the concerned citizens. The problem you get into is whether the free coffee or lunch constitutes a future conflict of interest.

Having someone buy you a doughnut or bowl of soup isn't a conflict. The nature of most people who hold public office is to gladly accept such free gifts. My advice is to shun the offers, not rudely, but to stay neutral.

For example, I show up first for coffee or lunch. I order my own food. That way, I don't feel beholden to any person or group.

The offer of free coffee or food made in exchange for a favorable decision down the road may not be the intent of the well-meaning mover or shaker. Still, be on guard for such things. My hope is that your decisions are made to benefit the public, not a few special interests.

The Quasi-Judicial Role

The three branches of American government are executive, legislative, and judicial. This organization is consistent down to the local level, where often a legislative body like a city council is required to assume a judicial role. The terminology used is *quasi-judicial.*

» At the local level, the executive branch can be an elected official, such as a mayor, but is often hired staff: an executive director, administrator, or superintendent, for example.

» Any council or board operates as a legislative body, making policy decisions for the organization.

» Local government operates without a designated judicial branch, which is why the legislative body is called upon to operate in a quasi-judicial manner.

Becoming judge and jury

Certain matters that come before a local governing board are judicial in nature. This stipulation is made by code or the circumstances of the decision: A hearing is held and evidence is admitted at the hearing. It's up to the legislative board, acting in a quasi-judicial manner, to weigh the evidence presented and adjudicate a decision.

The quasi-judicial hearing is different from a typical public hearing, which is often labeled a legislative hearing. Both types of hearings proceed in similar steps:

1. The hearing is opened.

2. Both sides make a presentation, pro and con.

3. Individuals offer testimony in favor, opposed, or neutral.

4. Follow-up, rebuttal, or closing arguments are offered.

5. The body deliberates, coming to a decision.

Before deliberation (Step 5), elected officials can ask questions and make clarifications. Only after all the evidence is submitted does the body discuss the issue and arrive at a decision.

For a quasi-judicial hearing, it's vital that the decision made is based solely on the evidence presented during the hearing. The goal is to ensure that all elected officials sitting as judge and jury have access to the same information. See the later section "Avoiding *ex parte* communications."

>> Quasi-judicial matters require full disclosure of any conflicts of interest. Refer to the earlier section "Conflicts of Interest."

>> A quasi-judicial hearing means you're making a ruling based on evidence presented during the hearing.

>> Legislative hearings are required for certain issues based on code. Unlike quasi-judicial hearings, information outside of what's presented can also be weighed for the decision.

>> The format for a quasi-judicial hearing may differ from what's presented in this section.

>> A quasi-judicial hearing may also be held to appeal a judicial decision made by staff or a city committee.

>> Not every issue that rises before you is a hearing. The public is often surprised to learn that they can't comment on certain matters as they're presented. Therefore, many agencies offer public comment as a way for the public to provide feedback on nonhearing items. See Chapter 17.

Avoiding ex parte communications

The success of a quasi-judicial hearing relies upon the legislative body having equal access to the evidence. When you have information beyond what's presented at the meeting, the detail is considered *ex parte*, which is Latin for "from the side."

To avoid *ex parte* communications, follow these rules:

>> You cannot interview people involved. On your own, you can't contact any party involved in the hearing. You cannot listen to their arguments outside of the hearing.

>> You cannot have access to evidence outside of the hearing. This means if someone contacts you with some information, you must shun the call. Instead, urge the person to comment at the hearing and present the evidence.

>> You cannot do your own research. For example, don't do a site visit to a property being considered for modification. Yes, even driving by the site for a quick look-see is giving yourself access to information others won't have.

>> You cannot discuss the issue with others. If a citizen phones you to rant about the issue, immediately inform them that you aren't allowed to discuss it. Be firm. Encourage them to come to the hearing and state their case.

>> Above all, you cannot discuss the hearing with other elected officials. Though you can say, "Big hearing tonight," you cannot say, "What do you think about that annexation?"

The result of for engaging in *ex parte* communications is that one party is denied a fair hearing. The penalty is that your agency can be sued. This reason is why your agency attorney should brief you on specific rules regarding quasi-judicial hearings. This information should be part of your training packet; refer to the earlier section "Orientation."

If you have access to *ex parte* information, ensure that you disclose it at the start the hearing. For example, you can announce that you live near the subject property and drive by it every day. Or mention that you know an applicant, though you haven't discussed the item with them.

When in doubt regarding any issue, consult with the agency's attorney.

Your Role

Government is just full of surprises, especially for someone who wins an election after a political career of criticizing elected officials. Suddenly you discover that the roles are narrowly defined. The infinite power you thought awaited you isn't to be found.

>> Government officials have powers, not rights. The list of powers you have is enumerated and short. Outside of a public meeting, you pretty much have zero power.

>> Even monarchs and dictators have limited powers. When appointed dictator for life, Julius Caesar was frustrated with the slow pace by which his reforms were implemented.

Serving the public

Your first duty as an elected official is to serve the public. Your role in the organization is to represent the people. It's not to represent the administration or staff. You are the people's representative in the machine.

Though you were hired by the people, still you're considered a government employee. You may have a salary, benefits, a staff, and an office, though at the local level these perks are limited. The organization cannot fire you; only the public has that opportunity should you decide to run again.

As a member of the organization, you are not answerable to the staff or other elected officials. For example, city council members don't work for the mayor, and school board trustees don't work for the superintendent.

DAN SAYS

>> Other elected officials cannot tell you what to do. Yes, they may crow seniority or remind you that it's "tradition" to do something. Unless they can point to a policy, adopted at a public meeting, that gives one elected official power over another, they're full of crap.

>> In a large legislative body, roles may be defined where some elected officials do have seniority over others. This situation is rare at the local level, where an elected body is small and not as snooty.

>> I view the role of the elected official as being a supercitizen. You have all the rights a mortal citizen has, but as a member of the organization, you have personal access to specific parts of the machine. You can help people navigate the bowels of the beast, get answers faster, and ask questions that receive more attention than a regular citizen.

>> Signing a loyalty oath is not part of your role as an elected official. When I was first elected to the city council, the mayor (who did not trust me) insisted that I sign an oath of allegiance to the city administrator. I refused. Further, I went to the press because I thought such a thing was obnoxious. I represent the people, not the damn administrator.

Accepting limitations on your infinite power

As a longtime city councilman, I can cite only two powers I have:

1. I can place an item on an agenda for discussion.

2. I can vote during a noticed meeting on agenda action items.

That's it. That's my infinite power, and it's pretty much the infinite power most elected officials have at the local level. In fact, in some jurisdictions you may not be allowed to set agenda items. (Check with the agency attorney, and then check again because many of them are unsure.)

Your second (or only) power is wielded at a public meeting. The meeting must be noticed. The public must be allowed to attend. The agenda must be published in advance and cannot be modified after publication or can be modified only under certain emergency circumstances.

Your power manifests itself as one vote: Yes or no, aye or nay. A majority of your peers must vote the same for you to get your way. That's the power you have in a legislative body, like a board of trustees or a town council.

>> If your elected position is administrative, you have no meetings and no power to vote. Your role is to implement the policy as stated in code. You can make administrative decisions and staff decisions, and you can hobnob like you're really important.

>> A city mayor can be considered an administrative position, legislative position, or both. For example, the mayor may vote along with other members of council, may be allowed to vote only to break a tie, or may not be allowed to vote at all.

Making policy versus administrative roles

In a legislative role, such as town council or school board trustee, your job is to make policy. You set the rules by which the organization runs.

In an administrative role, such as mayor, your function is to implement the policy set by the legislative body. In this role, you can direct staff to perform certain tasks to fulfill policy as set by the legislative body.

These two roles, policy-maker and administrator, must not cross.

For example, as a school board trustee, you cannot personally direct any staff member to do anything. To do so puts them in an awkward spot because they want to respect you, though they cannot obey such a direct order. The only way you can direct staff is to set an item on an agenda and persuade a majority of your peers to vote with you to direct staff.

Similar restrictions apply to an administrative position. Though a mayor or another elected administrator can direct staff to perform tasks, they can't make instant policy decisions. To address an issue that isn't in code or doesn't exist in the current policy manual, the legislative body must meet to form a new policy.

>> Before you go on a policy-setting binge, ask staff about those issues that concern you. "What is being done about the lack of art supplies?" Study up on the issue, and then ask staff what you can do to help.

DAN SAYS

>> An approach I use to avoid directing staff is to phrase the request in the form of a question. Rather than order staff, "Fix the potholes on Atlas Road," which I have no power to order, I ask, "When will the potholes on Atlas Road be fixed?" It's a nondirective, innocent question, one that any citizen can ask.

Cooperation

Allow yourself time to become familiar with your elected position, just as you would approach anything new. Keep in mind that staff and other electeds may have reservations about you. They may be hesitant to trust you until they get to know you — or they may never trust you.

In today's divisive, acidic political climate, you have no reason to bring animosity and anger to local office. You may disagree with your peers, but don't hate them for it. Hopefully, they'll return the same respect. Truculent, nasty elected officials rarely see a second term.

Remember that you've joined a moving train. People don't like change, and *you* are the change. Good change takes time, so build some trust and cooperation.

>> Be civil with fellow electeds. If you get angry or short, ensure that you quickly and publicly apologize.

>> Don't take animosity against your peers to social media. The effect is to make the entire organization look bad.

>> You don't have to suck up to another elected official. No matter how long they've been in office or how much more popular they are than you, on the dais you are equals.

>> Especially at the low levels, be nice to staff. Your kindness will be remembered.

>> Always cut people some slack. Be the adult. Be the big brother or sister. Don't let petty issues grow to the point where you become the focus of a viral YouTube video of a public meeting. Bad behavior hurts you *and* the organization.

Chapter **16**

Public Service

Your new position working for the government as an elected official is about customer service. You represent the public. You must also work well with staff. To pull off a good stint in office and be successful, you must manage both.

DAN SAYS

» You are the public's representative, not their boss or leader.

» I believe the role of an elected official is to protect the rights of the people. This must be your first concern.

The Staff

The day-to-day operations of government are carried out by people I collectively refer to as *staff*. These are paid government employees who fill specific roles and do the work that government sets out to accomplish.

Staff may be initially cautious around you, especially if you're not well known or specifically if you ran on a platform to reduce staff. Eventually, they'll warm up. Your desire is to build a healthy, happy, and productive relationship with the people who actually do the work.

Knowing who's who

If you haven't yet met with key staff members before you ran for office, do so now. It's important that you know their names, faces, and positions. The organization has various department heads, chiefs, superintendents, and supervisors. Know who is who.

It helps to understand the organization's structure. How is the work divided? For example, a school district may have one director of curriculum or two — one for upper grades and the other for elementary grades. An organizational chart should be available to help you navigate the organization's hierarchy.

Ensure that you visit with all department heads or chiefs. If you're told to meet with only the administrator, rebuff that admonition. You can't understand how the organization works until you meet the people who actually do the work. I strongly recommend you speak with staff at all levels, not only as an introduction but frequently afterward.

Ask staff which they prefer: a planned visit or a random drop-in. Some staff may become alarmed when you set a planned visit, thinking something is wrong. Others may be too busy to devote time to you if you just stop by to see what's up. Regardless, always ask the staffer if they have a few minutes before you plop down in their office.

During your meetings, planned or unannounced, remember that staff is forced to respect you. (Well, technically they respect the public who thrust you into office.) They will address you formally. They will drop everything when you come to visit. That's a lot of power; use it wisely to benefit the public, not because you enjoy getting smoke blown up your skirt.

DAN SAYS

>> Want to be a better elected official? Talk with the staff!

>> I meet with not only top-level staff but worker bees as well. I stop by and ask, "What's going on?" They're happy to explain what they do and offer other insights about the organization. They'll appreciate your attentiveness.

>> If the rules are strict and you're informed that elected officials aren't allowed to randomly visit with the staff, take heed. You might ask for clarification from an administrator on why such a rule is necessary. Further, check with the organization's attorney to see whether breaking the rule is a major offense.

TIP

>> Staff routinely hold meetings or have special occasions where employees are honored, promotions given, or presentations made. Show up to as many of these events as you can. It means a lot to the workers when elected officials take the time to get involved.

>> Honestly, the only way you'll ever truly know what's going on with the organization is to meet with staff.

Assigning department liaisons

Some local governments assign elected officials as liaisons to specific departments. For example, on the city council you may be assigned to the police, building inspection, and street maintenance departments. These become the departments with which you interface and do whatever other tasks are required.

When department liaisons are assigned, ensure that you don't step on toes by interacting with other departments. Doing so can raise the ire of other elected officials. And you don't want them overstepping by interacting with your departments as well. Most of your peers respect this limitation.

DAN SAYS

I'm not a fan of department liaisons. It really limits your effectiveness by hindering your interaction with all of government. For example, if a citizen calls you asking why a street didn't get plowed, you need not shy away because Councilman Anderson is the streets liaison.

Interacting with staff

As a member of a legislative body, you cannot direct staff to do anything. For example, when Betty Jane Chronic calls, asking the city to paint the curb red in front of her house, you cannot tell the street painter to do so. No, such a request is carried out by staff based on established policy and scheduling. What you can do, however, is ask questions.

Any member of the public can ask a question, but as the supercitizen, you'll get a faster response. Further, you have better access.

When you know the answer, get back to the citizen — this is customer service. Say, "Betty, your street is scheduled to be painted in three weeks. I'll call back to remind you so that you can ensure the cat is inside."

REMEMBER

>> Your interaction with staff is for the benefit of the public.

>> Staff should provide you with an answer unless a policy is in place that forbids them from doing so. As a policy maker, however, keep in mind that you can alter the policy if you believe it to be silly or counterproductive.

>> Do not ask staff for favors.

>> Do not perform favors for staff. If you have a concern, raise it with the administrator or place it on an agenda for discussion.

>> Respect the chain of command. It's okay to ask questions of the worker bees, but if you have questions regarding how a department is run, meet with the department head.

>> Be assertive, not aggressive. You're entitled to answers to your questions.

>> If you have an issue with a staff member, bring it to the proper channel. In nearly every case, that would be the organization's administrator. Don't try to handle conflicts on your own. Don't make threats.

Avoiding surprises

Like everyone else who suffers in a complex system, government employees don't like change. They prefer calm, predictable waters. One of the things you can do to negatively affect the consistency is to inject a surprise into the mix. No one in government likes surprises.

The theory holds that if you don't surprise staff, they won't surprise you. They'll keep you informed and in the loop on what's going on. Likewise, you tell them what you're thinking and they'll repay the kindness.

For example, if a meeting is pending and I have questions on an agenda item, I email a potential list of questions to the staffer making the presentation, carbon-copying other interested parties. My point isn't to get the answers outside of the meeting, but to let them know what questions might be raised so that they can have an answer ready.

If I don't send an email, I meet with the staffer in person, which is less formal and perhaps a more approachable method. I often learn more.

The point is to avoid a surprise. Staff likes the input. Though they may have had plenty of meetings and discussions already, your questions may raise issues no one has thought of. They'll appreciate the heads-up.

WARNING

>> Surprises still happen. For example, you may think of a brilliant question during a meeting for which staff is unprepared to answer. Remember, you can table an item for later discussion, but you need a majority of your peers to agree with such an action.

>> Never pull a "gotcha" on staff. It doesn't matter what you're trying to do in the big picture — the effect will render you useless as an elected official, because no staff member will trust you again.

>> Treat staff well and they'll repay the kindness.

Members of the Public

Your employers are members of the public — everyone who lives in the district you represent. Yes, even those people who voted against you and claim that you're not their trustee (or whatever) and utter foul statements about you and your hairstyle. All these are the people you represent.

DAN SAYS

Indeed, it may surprise you that should you become an effective elected official, those who obviously did not support you will contact you for assistance. Help them as best you can. A good politician never dismisses someone for having a one-time lack of insight.

Serving your constituents

Of all the things you'll do in office, one key theme ties everything together: Represent the public. That's what people expect of you. You are a public servant.

Your contact information — perhaps even your personal cell phone number — becomes part of your public record. When you get a call, answer. If you can't answer at once, respond later. Reply to all your email. These simple acts are what's required to be good at your job.

Alas, you can't have an answer for everything. Too many people want government to play the Mommy-and-Daddy role. For example, you get a call that a neighbor's firepit is blowing smoke into the baby's window. Honestly, there's little you can do but listen. Staff will inform you of any codes violated, and staff enforces the code. Still, for taking the call — or paying a personal visit —you're doing what's expected of you.

If, on the other hand, you avoid returning calls or answering emails, don't be surprised if your perception is diminished in the public. They'll grumble, "Trustee Hornwood doesn't seem to care," and they're right. By shutting down communications, you come across as aloof.

REMEMBER

>> Keep your phone number public, even if it means getting a separate cell phone.

>> Take notes during a call. First, write down the citizen's name and the date and time. Ensure that you get back to them, even if nothing significant has transpired. People don't call politicians unless they're truly frustrated.

>> You represent *all* the people, not just people who supported you, people who are your friends or beer buddies, or those wine-and-cheese supporters.

>> Serving the public doesn't imply that you must agree with every constituent all the time. Your task is to do what's best for most, which is ugly, but it's how the system works.

>> Some problems are unsolvable, yet you'll find yourself dragged into them anyway. For example, the issue may be with another government agency or between an individual and a business. When you return such calls, you find yourself as a sounding board for a disgruntled individual. That's fine, though keep reminding them that the situation is outside of what you can do as an elected official.

Following through

The key to success for communications as an elected official is follow-through. It's something you must excel at.

Follow-through means not only replying to an email but also making a note of the conversation and checking back later. It's especially important that you do so even if you have nothing to report. If you fail to communicate, people feel they're being ignored. Therefore, even a no-news update is appreciated.

You know that you've become successful at follow-through when you have a reputation for being the first to respond, to answer email, to return a phone call. It's delightful to overhear a conversation or observe on social media someone suggesting that they give you a call because you always respond.

Public Communications

You can use your campaign's old communications tools to keep your supporters informed after you're elected. Or if you didn't have a campaign communication tool, start one as an elected official. This technique is yet another way you can go the extra mile to maintain communications.

Consider sending out an electronic missive or newsletter at least once per quarter. Do so more frequently for hot-button issues that come up during the year.

Use the communications to let the public know what's going on with the agency. Things are always happening, so choose from the list one or more of those items that you feel will affect the public: new schools opening, road closures, committee openings, and so on.

One goal of your communications is to avoid the common question "When was the government going to tell us this?" Indeed, try as it can, government is quite poor at communications. Even agencies with public information officers recognize that communicating with the public is an ongoing task.

>> The list of contacts in your communications database is gold should you consider running for reelection.

>> One choice you might consider for keeping in touch is Constant Contact. It's a paid service, but it works well at managing email lists and helping you market your message: constantcontact.com.

The Press

It's important that you understand the role the press plays in government. They're the watchdog, though at the local level, few small governments are routinely if ever covered by the press. Still, that doesn't make the press any less of a player.

>> The press, and media in general, are a tool that can work for you and against you. Don't expect them to always be on your side. Likewise, don't act surprised when they are. Knowing how to deal with the press is important.

DAN SAYS

>> The smaller the political body, the easier it tends toward corruption. The media prefers that we look to the statehouse or to Washington. Yet just down the road, and thanks to a lack of interest by the press, local elected officials routinely ride roughshod over the law.

Developing a positive relationship with the media

When a reporter calls, you answer the phone. Doing so builds a level of trust, which causes them to phone you more often. The result is getting your name in the paper, which adds to your exposure and helps should you decide to run again.

When you can't take the call, ensure that you return it as soon as possible. By then, it's usually too late, because they've contacted someone else, but you show that their call is important.

REMEMBER

When talking with a reporter, keep in mind that everything you say is on the record. Everything. You can't say, "Off the record, Mike, I saw the mayor take the money from the Sunday collection plate." That's not off the record — it's a story and the reporter will go for it.

Never lie to the press. Lying about something always makes matters worse. It's okay to say you don't remember. It's also okay to say that you'll get back to the reporter later. And if you don't want to answer a question, don't. Or use the time-honored political trick of answering a question that wasn't asked. But don't lie.

Some matters are internal to the organization and shouldn't be discussed. You may be briefed by the agency's attorney not to discuss a pending lawsuit or personnel matter. If asked by a reporter, immediately direct them to contact the agency's attorney. Say, "I've been instructed not to comment on this issue." They'll understand.

Finally, expect to be misquoted. You may think you're offering up Pulitzer Prize–winning material but then find that your only quote is not only poorly worded but also incorrect. It happens all the time. Just let it roll.

Tossing a reporter a bone

One way to use the press to your advantage is to give them stories. They may not write about everything, but when something concerns you, give a reporter a call. Let them know what's going on and why you think it's going to be a big deal.

The reporter may not go with your suggestion. That's fine, but don't let rejection dissuade you from trying again. Eventually, you may find reporters calling you and asking whether you know about anything coming up. Because you're a good elected official and you communicate well with staff and know what's happening at the organization, you should be able to feed the reporter a nice narrative in which they can find a story.

Being caught off guard

Hopefully, staff keeps you informed, especially regarding emergencies and sudden events. The goal is to prep you should the press call. It's embarrassing when the press or a member of the public phones to alert you of some event related to your agency and you haven't a clue what's going on. I know.

The primary purpose of the heads-up is to avoid your being caught off guard. You must have a response ready, which includes the agency's standard response but perhaps your own comments as well — if allowed. Keep in mind that some events involve current or potential litigation, in which case the only allowed response is to have the reporter contact the agency's attorney.

Another way to be caught off guard is when you've been naughty or accused of such and a reporter calls you to get your take. For this stressful incident, you have several options.

Your first choice is to explain that you haven't heard anything or to claim that you must ask around and call back the reporter. If so, definitely ask around to see what's up, formulate a response, and then get back to the reporter.

A second choice is to deal with the call, especially if you're aware of the situation and, as a smart person, have already formulated a response. Stay calm. Avoid emotion. Be factual.

Any further choices you make slide you into the circle of doubt regardless of the incident's nature. For example, you don't have to take the call at all. In that case, the press reports that you were "unavailable for comment." Such a statement coming from an elected official rarely has a bouquet-of-roses aroma.

You can also be dodgy, which reporters love because it gives them more latitude to write ugly prose about you. For instance, they ask whether you used campaign funds for personal expenses and you reply, "I took money from friends and supporters. . .." This isn't an answer, and the reporter will sense your dodge instantly.

>> As a public official, anyone can fabricate anything about you, though rarely will it happen. (Actually, if it does, it means you must be tweaking some high-and-mighty jerk's nose.) Rarely, however, at the local level does the public cast bald-faced lies at elected officials.

>> Review your SWOT chart from Chapter 6 to get an idea of how to handle potential moments where you can be caught off guard.

>> Never lie to the press.

Your Behavior in Public

Those humble hours between gavel slams are pretty much your own, but not really. As an elected official, you're effectively on the clock 24 hours a day, all week, every month, your entire term. Especially to the politically aware class, you are being watched.

My rule is to always pretend that someone is watching me. They have a camera. Further, they don't like me much. They're waiting for me to do something that will complete their universe and demonstrate to the greater public what a scumbag I am. This description may sound extreme, but I have several such stalkers, even in my own small town.

Of course, you're human. Your temper will flare someday. You'll snap at a kid in the grocery store, yell at a driver who cut you off, or do any of hundreds of awkward things regular people do every day. Just remember that someone could be watching and you may have to deal with a letter to the editor or a comment at a public meeting about how you failed, for example, to use your turn signal.

Other, more unpleasant regular life incidents are magnified when you hold an elected office. The sheriff may have conducted two dozen DUI arrests over the weekend and no one cares, but if yours was one of them, prepare for the fallout. A speeding ticket in a school zone may make the news. Anything negative happening with your business becomes fodder for the local gossip mill. These and similar incidents become the dandruff that settles upon your shoulders as a public figure.

TIP

>> Always dress the part, or at least as much as you can. If you attend a meeting or even an informal coffee, dress professionally. Yes, you can have casual days, but people expect more from elected officials.

>> Get a dashcam for your car. Should any road incident occur, the dashcam provides an independent observation of events.

>> Being on your best behavior in public isn't as difficult as it sounds. Everyone should strive to be friendly in a public space — smile, say hello, be nice. Don't be surprised when random people greet you. Say hello back or, better, say "Nice to see you again," even if you don't remember who they are.

- » **Making meetings public**
- » **Creating public records**
- » **Minding your meeting behavior**
- » **Honoring citizen input**
- » **Maintaining your public record**

Chapter **17**

At a Public Meeting

You've attended meetings before, such as the boring ones at work, civic organization meetings, association meetings, and casual get-togethers. You've also attended public meetings, where you sit quietly and ponder why things move so slowly, why people avoid asking obvious questions, and how some elected officials can speak for so long and not say a darn thing. Yet it's all quite different when you perch on the dais yourself and partake of the action (or lack of action) from the point of view of an elected official.

Transparency

The public's business must take place in public in as transparent a manner as possible. This description means that all documents, communications, and other information are available to the public, either directly or upon request.

Transparency implies that your actions as an elected official are obvious and in the open when it comes to decisions made about the organization.

> » You and your agency can be as transparent as glass and some folks still accuse you of hiding things. It's the nature of the American public to be distrustful of government.

>> Most of transparency's effect is built upon reputation. If the agency has been known to be sneaky, following only the minimums for public disclosure, rebuilding a reputation will take time.

>> State law covers transparency in government. These laws may be referred to as open-meeting laws or open-meeting acts. In California, the Brown Act deals with transparency in government.

>> The big issue with transparency is a lack of enforcement.

>> Government transparency doesn't extend into your life and business. Though you're an elected official, you still have a personal right to privacy.

Keeping the public's business public

Most states and localities have specific laws to ensure that the public's business remains in public. Often, two sets of laws work side-by-side: One is the public-records law, which allows the public to examine or copy any public record or document. The second is the open-meeting law, which ensures that government business is conducted in full and fair view of the public.

The public-records laws are touched upon in the next section. For the conduct of meetings, the purpose of the open-meeting law is to ensure that the public is fully aware of what the government is doing and that all decisions take place in a well-noticed, transparent manner. For example:

Meetings must be noticed. Decisions take place only at meetings where full notice is given for the public, time and location, usually several days in advance.

Access must be available to the meeting. The meeting must be held in a place accessible to the public.

A quorum of elected officials must be present. The meeting can't take place unless a sufficient number of elected officials is present. Called a *quorum,* its size is set by code.

An agenda must be published. The discussion topics and potential action items for the government body must be known in advance. Restrictions may prohibit or limit items that can be added to the agenda after it's published.

Serial and secret meetings are prohibited. A quorum of elected officials cannot meet outside of the meeting to discuss or deliberate any issue coming before the body. This discussion includes phone calls and emails and meeting with each other one at a time for the purpose of deliberation outside of the public's view.

You should be familiar with the specific open-meeting laws that apply to your organization. The agency's attorney may have the details for you, and they were probably provided during your orientation.

The organization's clerk or administrator is in charge of ensuring that the open-meeting laws are followed.

>> Violation of any of these rules results in an illegal meeting and the decisions made rendered void. Your state may also levy punitive damages on elected officials for knowingly or repeatedly violating the open-meeting laws.

>> *Quorum* is the Latin plural for "of whom."

>> A quorum is typically a majority of the elected officials in a body. Exactly half the officials may or may not be counted as a quorum. For city councils, the mayor may or may not be counted as part of the quorum.

>> Holding a meeting behind closed doors, even if the public can hear and see the meeting, would be considered a violation of the open-meeting law.

>> It might be considered okay to discuss potential issues with your fellow elected officials, though only in numbers fewer than a quorum. Even then, it's best that you delay discussion until the meeting so that any decision takes place in full view of the public.

>> Matters of a quasi-judicial nature cannot be discussed among members of the body before the hearing. Refer to Chapter 15.

Creating a paper trail

Part of transparency ensures that public documents are available to the public. Outside a short list of excluded items (see the next section), just about every printed piece of paper and communications is considered a public document, which any member of the public can request to examine or have a copy made.

Commonly called the public-records law, or less frequently by the Federal term Freedom of Information Act, the laws in your state govern which documents are available and how they can be obtained.

Of primary concern is that your email account at the agency is subject to a public-records request. Essentially, any email you send or reply to is a public record. For this reason, always assume when you compose email that it will be read by someone else in the future. Be careful.

Further, you may discover that your private communications may be subject to public disclosure if you conduct public business using your personal email account or even send a text message. Your agency's attorney can fill you in on the details.

My advice is to assume that someone is reading everything you write. Further, to be safe, never reply to a government inquiry by using your personal email. If you receive a message regarding public business on your private account, immediately forward it to your government email and then reply.

Avoid text messages regarding public business, because your phone may become discoverable in a court case. In fact, the best policy is never to text another elected official or send a message regarding public business by using your phone.

» You took advantage of the public-records law when you obtained voter information for your campaign, as described in Chapter 7.

» Check with the agency's attorney regarding policies about private email and text messages.

» The best way to discuss an issue where you don't want a paper trail is over the phone or in person. This approach doesn't imply that you're being dodgy or skirting the public-record laws. It's just wise policy.

Excluding items from the public

Not every government document is considered a public record available for view by anyone. Some records are restricted, mostly for legal and privacy reasons. These items are mentioned in the law, though you should become familiar with the type of restricted documents and understand why they aren't available as public records.

Typical items excluded from a public-records request include personnel matters, details on pending legal action, property purchases and sales, and other items that may become public in the future but, for the agency's legal protection, cannot be disclosed.

Excluding items from the public also applies to open meetings. For example, if the school district is going to negotiate price for a piece of property upon which to build an elementary school, it's best done privately. These matters can be noticed as "property negotiation" in a general sense, but the presentation is made in what's commonly called executive session or a closed-door meeting.

The list of items that can be discussed in executive session are outlined in code. Further rules may apply as well, such as no deliberations or voting in executive session.

It's important that you do not abuse executive session. The temptation is ripe because when you're behind closed doors who knows what you're doing? Hopefully your administrator or agency attorney provides solid guidance and admonishes the body when it steps outside of what's allowed beyond view of the public.

Disclosing conflicts and recusing yourself

Transparency falls upon you when it comes to fully disclosing any conflicts you have with a pending issue. In most cases, announcing your conflict before the discussion is all it takes.

For example, you could say, "I know the applicant, who has been a friend for several years. I don't feel my personal relationship with him will conflict with my ability to make a fair decision." If the agency's attorney is good with that declaration, you can continue. Keep in mind, however, that public perception may be different. In fact, the old adage is that when you feel a conflict exists, one does.

When you're conflicted, recuse yourself from the discussion item. Suppose that the issue involves a company you work for. If the company gets the government contract, you'll receive a bonus. Voting in favor of this contract is a definite conflict, so you make an announcement at the start of discussion: "I work for the applicant and therefore shall recuse myself from this item."

After announcing your recusal, get up and leave the dais. If you can, leave the room. Don't editorialize before you leave. Don't just push back your chair and pretend to look disinterested. Get out.

When the presentation, deliberation, and voting are complete, you can return to your place on the dais and continue with the meeting.

The Public Meeting

As a member of a legislative body, a town council, or a board of trustees, you hold power only when a quorum is present at a public meeting. This time is when items are raised for discussion, in which you participate, and eventually vote, where you can exercise one of your powers as an elected official.

Meetings are not to be free-for-alls. They're organized and follow an agenda. The conduct of the meeting is set by code but also by local policy and tradition. To be an effective elected official, you must work within the framework provided to enact the change you want to seek.

DAN SAYS

>> The purpose of the meeting is to conduct the people's business in the presence of the people.

>> Government meetings must be noticed.

>> The meeting's agenda must be published.

>> Action takes place only on agenda action items when a quorum of officials is present.

>> There is no solvable problem that a group of politicians can't render insolvable.

Setting the agenda

Meeting agendas are set in advance, first to inform the public of what business will be discussed and also to provide time for staff to ready any reports and presentations.

Most of the agenda items are routine. For example, a typical public meeting starts with these items:

1. Call to order

2. Roll call

3. Pledge of Allegiance

4. Changes to the agenda

5. Declared conflicts

6. Approval of the minutes

Variations exist; for example, the organization may have an invocation. Minutes might be included in a general-order item called the *consent calendar*.

Other items on the agenda include old business, new business, hearings, possibly an executive or closed-door session, and adjournment.

At some point before the meeting, the agenda is set. For the most part, staff places items on the agenda. These items require approval by the board or input for further direction.

Elected officials can also set items on the agenda, though the rules vary. In the best world, any elected official can place any item they desire on an agenda for discussion. The process is set by the organization's policy, which outlines how an agenda item is set.

For example, two elected officials may be required to request an item be placed on the agenda. The agenda item may require approval of the mayor. The issue may need to be vetted by the organization's attorney. Regardless, some described method for setting agenda items must be available for you to peruse.

During the meeting, the agenda can be altered, but only under specific circumstances. Usually, the new item must be some form of emergency. In fact, an emergency rule may be in place where a quick meeting can be called without notice. It's rare for such a thing to happen, but emergency rules are available.

>> A *consent calendar* is a clutch of common items passed as a single motion. These items are routine, such as the payment of bills, minutes, and other items that lack controversy or don't require deliberation.

>> It's possible to alter the order of items as the meeting progresses. For example, you could make a motion to move a hot-button topic to the top of the agenda, especially when the angry mob shows up.

>> If you're told that you have no power to place an item on the agenda or that you must first go through some sort of ordeal, confirm such a policy is in line with existing code. It's rude but common for haughty elected officials and administrators to desire to throttle some discussion items and, specifically, some elected officials. Ensure that they're standing on solid ground if they turn you down.

DAN SAYS

>> At my city council training, we were informed that any council member can place an item on the agenda. When I attempted to do so, I was rebuffed by the administrator who said it was only the mayor who had that power. Confused, I challenged the decision. I was later told by an outside authority that it's a "city council meeting," not the "mayor's meeting," and that any council member can set an agenda item. Always stand up for yourself, which means you're standing up for the people who sent you into office.

>> Once you set an item on the agenda, no other elected official or staff can remove it.

Conducting yourself during a meeting

The public meeting is run by a designated individual, such as a chairman, president, or mayor. This person's job is to ensure that business is conducted in an orderly manner. The goal is to give everyone an opportunity to speak and discuss items and not have the meeting degenerate into a dysfunctional family picnic.

Your organization may have official meeting procedures, but at the local level, things progress according to tradition. Robert's Rules aren't adopted for the meeting, though the general process of making a motion, getting a second, and so on are followed.

Without exception, you cannot speak unless called upon by the chair. Use whatever method is standard to be recognized, such as activating a light on your microphone or raising a finger. When you're called, thank the chair and proceed with your comments or question. Speaking without being recognized is disruptive.

The items you speak about are related to the agenda item under consideration. I encourage you to ask questions, even if you already know the answer. The purpose is transparency, but also to inform the public. Nothing is more irritating to me than watching a public meeting where the officials don't ask innocent or obvious questions. Such practice makes the meeting look rehearsed.

Keep your discussion focused. It's easy to get into the weeds and off topic. The agency's attorney or clerk may attempt to refocus you, though many don't do so, out of respect for your position. If you like, ask the clerk, "Would the clerk please remind the body of the current discussion topic?"

You cannot bring up or discuss items not on the agenda. If an opportunity is given for elected officials to comment, you can editorialize. But don't expect anything you say to evolve into a deliberation on an off-agenda topic. The meeting chair will help keep you focused.

Speak up if the chair hasn't recognized you and you still want to speak. You have authority to deliberate, even if the other electeds don't like you and do sneaky things to prevent you from talking.

When it comes time to vote, you do so by voice vote or roll call. For a voice vote, the body says "Aye" or "Nay" as a group. The chair calls the winner. For local government, most votes are voice votes and the results are pretty much always unanimously *aye*.

A roll call vote must occur for specific items, as outlined in code. Further, you may have the authority to demand a roll call vote as a privilege. If so, the clerk or another official reads the roll and you vote after your name is called, *aye* or *nay*.

You can also request a roll call vote if you feel the chair has improperly called a voice vote.

It's rare, but seldom if ever are you allowed to vote by secret ballot. In fact, I know of no state that allows elected officials to decide issues in this manner.

TIP

>> *Robert's Rules of Order* is a collection of meeting rules and procedures as well as a book of the same name. You don't need to purchase this book or memorize its rules. I can, however, recommend as a good primer *Robert's Rules For Dummies*, written by C. Alan Jennings (Wiley).

>> Truth be told, following Robert's Rules for a small deliberative body is a pain. Please don't be one of those freshly minted elected officials who quotes Robert's Rules at everyone.

>> Most legislative bodies follow *Mason's Manual of Legislative Procedure*, not Robert's Rules.

>> If you vote against the crowd, please spell out your reason. After the motion is made and seconded, the chair should ask for further discussion. At that point, explain your vote. The public may not agree with you, but they will appreciate that you explained why you're voting against something.

>> Stay off your damn cell phone during the meeting. Trust me: You're not good enough to make it look like you're not on your cell phone. Just mute it and put it away.

>> Not every issue requires debate. Most items are routine, and everyone votes yes. Don't feel like you always must pipe in with a comment.

DAN SAYS

>> I was at a meeting once that went so far afield one of the elected officials made a motion to suspend discussion and vote immediately. Fortunately, the chair didn't recognize this parliamentary trick and the item was discussed. Also see the nearby sidebar, "Crummy meeting maneuvers."

Attending workshops

A workshop is a less-formal version of an official government meeting. Often, it's informational in nature, such as an extended discussion, a presentation, training, or another event that must be noticed as a meeting (because a quorum of elected officials is present), but it's not a regular business meeting.

Like a meeting, a workshop has a noticed agenda. It must be called to order, the roll read, and items discussed. The agenda may contain action items that require a vote. The meeting must be formally adjourned.

CRUMMY MEETING MANEUVERS

Some elected officials get cranky and desire to stifle deliberation on certain topics. A common way to shut down debate is to "call for the question." This motion, outlined in Robert's Rules, is designed to refocus the body when two individuals go back and forth with the intention of arguing rather than deliberating.

Calling for the question is abused when an elected official just wants to hurry up and vote. A good chair ignores such a request and asks whether anyone else has anything to offer. A bad chair immediately calls for a vote on the question (not on the issue). At that time, speak up and mention that you haven't yet deliberated. The chair may not agree with you, but at least you've made your point.

Another trick is to ask for unanimous consent. This item means that everyone will, by acclamation, agree to whatever has been proposed. This trick is used not for important items, but usually for inconsequential ones, where it's a desire for the body to come across as unified.

By no means must you agree to a unanimous consent request. When the chair should ask whether anyone objects, do so at that time. It doesn't make you a bad guy to object to a unanimous consent request.

Depending on who runs the workshop, you may be permitted to spontaneously ask questions or interrupt. Such discretion is up to the chair.

Concerned Citizens Want to Be Heard

Just because they were foolish enough to send you to office at the election is no reason to ignore them now. The public has a voice that must be heard. Most public meetings offer an opportunity for the public to speak. For me, it's the best part of the meeting because you never know what some people are going to say.

>> The public-comment portion of a meeting is different from citizens offering testimony during a hearing.

>> Also see Chapter 18 for more information on interacting with members of the public.

Holding public comment

Not every public meeting offers a slot for citizens to speak. I feel it a noble gesture when they do. Public participation validates the public process.

When a public-comment item is on the meeting agenda, the public has an opportunity to address the body, ask questions, or raise issues. This period isn't an opportunity to challenge individual officials or make allegations. Public comment isn't a debate.

Some agencies limit their public comment only to agenda items. Some limit the comment only to non-agenda items, which I find confusing. Regardless, if the public is given a chance to speak, let them speak.

During public comment, the chair calls for citizens to speak. Some agencies may require people to sign up first; others use a more free-form approach. And some agencies offer multiple opportunities for the public to speak.

Most citizen comment periods are timed; the citizen has a given number of minutes to say whatever is on their mind. During this time, the public is watching the behavior of elected officials. If you appear disinterested, look at your watch, or play with your computer, it will be noticed. Please respect the public.

If allowed, you can interact with the public to a certain degree. With the chair's permission, ask questions. You can promise to investigate an item further or to get back to the citizen, which they'll appreciate.

REMEMBER

>> It's rare for members of the public to attend a government meeting, especially for a local office. People who further go out of their way to make public comment are doing so from an extreme desire. Please be respectful.

>> If it's your desire to interact with the public during an agency meeting, arrange for a town hall. Due to the issues raised not being on an agenda, the body can't take any action, but you can take notes and get feedback.

>> Some states may prohibit the agency from requiring citizens to sign up for public comment. It's considered a form of intimidation.

Dealing with upset people

A classic instance of public comment is when someone is upset. They express frustration at trying to resolve some issue or express that they feel ignored. The worst thing you can do at this point is to further ignore the person.

Please ask upset citizens questions to help you further understand the issue. Ask staff questions to get another view on what's happening. If you agree with the citizen's point of view, say so.

It's good government practice, though sadly uncommon, to follow up with upset people. Investigate the problem and see whether a solution can be arranged. Most of the issues that upset people spawn from botched communications.

Above all, never dismiss an upset citizen as a crank. Even when the issue has been raised dozens of times and has become an obsession, elected officials come across as rude when they're dismissive of any member of the public.

REMEMBER

>> Sadly, you receive little credit for resolving a citizen's issue, though you'll receive endless scorn if you neglect it.

>> Never make snide comments, even in private, about chronically upset members of the public.

>> One of the reasons people complain about the same issue over and over is that they don't feel they're being heard. Another reason is that the citizen may indeed be 100 percent incorrect, but the elected officials lack the spine to confront them for being wrong. You can do so in a manner that's not patronizing, yet few officials try.

PUBLIC-COMMENT GOLD

I enjoy public comment. Unlike every other item on the agenda, public comment offers a surprise. When a citizen ambles forth, they could be praising some recent decision or be ready to dig into the government for something no one has ever heard of. It's truly a marvelous event.

Beyond concerned citizens, public comments come from some exciting and diverse individuals. Most obvious are the chronic complainers. Try as you can to appease them, they must bemoan one thing or another. Usually, they want some special treatment — something to be done beyond the scope of your agency or something that's just horrendously expensive.

Also common are the grandstanders and comedians. These people may appear to be wasting time, but I find them a refreshing break. Some people just don't get enough attention. And who knows: Maybe someday they'll run for office and win?

Your Public Record

The agency itself manages your public record with regard to communications and other items available to the public. For yourself, however, I recommend that you keep copies of your public record as a sort of scrapbooking exercise.

For example, keep newspaper clippings where you are quoted. If you make the front page, keep the entire page. You don't have to formally set these items in a scrapbook, but keep them as your own documentation of your public career.

Also make a note of meetings where you spoke up passionately about an issue — even if the item failed to pass. Definitely keep track of those items you introduce that do pass. Keep the minutes. If the video is available online, bookmark it or ask for your own copy.

This data documents your public record. It comes in handy for reminiscing purposes, or it can serve as presentation material when you're invited to speak publicly. More importantly, it can be used should you choose to run for reelection. See Chapter 19.

IN THIS CHAPTER

» **Voting on routine matters**

» **Reading the material**

» **Doing your homework**

» **Making someone unhappy**

» **Being decisive**

» **Casting your vote**

Chapter **18**

Decisions: Who to Tick Off?

Y ou may have waltzed into office on a campaign of wishy-washy promises, never committing yourself to one side or another of any issue. When you're elected, however, you can vote only *aye* or *nay*; voting *maybe* or *perhaps* isn't allowed.

Most of the time, decision-making is an innocent affair. Every so often, however, a decision comes before you that is going to upset someone. If you're fortunate, you'll encounter issues that upset lots of people, which is really the best part of holding public office: demonstrating to the public that you can stand up for something. Suddenly, the options of saying *aye* or *nay* become terrifyingly difficult.

The Same Ol' Same Ol'

From the local office all the way up to Congress, you vote *aye* on nearly everything. Indeed, without any evidence whatsoever, I'd say that most public office votes are unanimously in favor of whatever issue comes before them.

The popularity of the *aye* vote is due to the abundance of routine material that comes before the board. Most of these items are noncontroversial: approving the minutes, motion to adjourn, approval of budgeted spending items, and so on. It's this humdrum that explains why many people don't pay attention to the smaller political divisions.

Though these decisions are routine, I recommend that you avoid becoming lazy. Always read the minutes, specifically with an eye to look for mistakes. It's delightful when something is wrong in the minutes and you mention it at the meeting for correction. This action makes the other electeds seem foolish because they failed to notice the problem or, more likely, to read the minutes.

If you can demonstrate that you've read the packet, even the boring stuff, it shows the public that you have a good grasp of what's going on. It's also shows staff that you take your role seriously, which encourages them to be more thoughtful with their reports.

Homework for Every Decision

The nonroutine items on the agenda deserve special attention. Most of the heavy lifting will be done by staff, because they're charged with presenting the report and providing the information to assist your decision. Still, that doesn't mean you act as a rubber stamp to approve their recommendation. You must do your homework.

Start by reading the staff report. Do an initial first pass, making notes for things that don't make sense.

On your second pass, confirm that your questions aren't answered elsewhere in the staff report. Check the numbers to confirm that they add up or have been properly referenced from elsewhere. If they don't match up, make a note of it.

Check dates and timelines.

Once you have a notion of what's going on, direct your questions to staff. Ensure that you do this before the meeting. First, you want to understand the issue in order to make the best decision. Second, you don't want to surprise staff with a complex question that they're ill prepared to answer.

My experience shows that staff are delighted when an elected official shows interest in their work. When you stop by to ask questions in person, or send questions via email, they work hard to provide you with good answers.

During the meeting, feel free to ask the same questions you've already asked. The public wants to know as well, and staff will be happy to explain the details. If you have concerns, raise them. *Remember:* You are the decision-maker, but you need a majority of your peers to agree with you to get your way.

WARNING

Be wary of gathering information on quasi-judicial matters. Before the meeting, it's okay to ask staff questions about the process, but avoid specific questions on the issue at hand. Detailed information can be presented only during a quasi-judicial hearing. Refer to Chapter 15.

That "Difficult Decision"

Nothing irks me more than a local politician who bemoans that something is a "tough decision." Or they say, "I wrestled with this." Not only are they horrid at acting, they're not even telling the truth. The ordeal that this weak politician is facing is that their decision, either way, is going to tick off one of their friends or supporters. Don't be that elected official.

Decisions you make as an elected official affect people, most of the time without directly affecting you. The fallout from some major decisions is that one or more people will be disappointed with your choice. Though your intention is to make the best decision for the public, many won't be thrilled. That's the essence of a difficult decision.

People who run for office don't do so to become unpopular. When faced with a decision that can negatively impact people, you're putting your popularity on the line. That's really what's tough about the decision. So instead of saying, "This is a difficult decision" an honest elected official would say, "This decision is going to make me less popular."

The point is not to overthink what may turn out to be the one vote that terminates your political career. You were elected to make a decision, to vote *aye* or *nay*. Do your research, weigh all sides, listen to the public, and then cast your vote.

Most important is that you explain why you've voting the way you are. Smart people respect that. Petty-minded individuals who dislike you anyway won't care. Don't worry about them. Back up your decision with data, and then cast your vote.

REMEMBER

>> Most people who get elected just want to be popular and not do the job. So, yes, for them, making a decision that angers a supporter is quite tough. It's not. Yes or no. That's the decision.

>> Back up your vote with facts.

>> Review your campaign promises. Confirm that your vote jibes with what you promised. If you vote against a promise, you put your reputation on the line should you choose to run for reelection. The voters value consistency, even when they disagree with you.

DAN SAYS

>> Indeed, I've seen single votes ruin a local politician's career. Such elected officials are accused of not listening to the public, when in fact they merely disagree. The problem is made worse when they refuse to explain their position or do so in an awkward or condescending manner.

>> Avoid listening to emotional arguments. People can get all wound up and start speaking from passion without presenting facts. You must make your decision on the law and evidence, not on emotion. Politicians who vote emotionally appear irrational.

>> Try to show common sense. It seems to be lacking at so many levels of government.

The Vote

After the report is given, or the hearing testimony heard, deliberations begin. It's this time when you can make your observations, ask further questions, and discuss the merits of the issue.

The discussion on an item is never a true debate — and you don't want it to be. You want to offer opinions. If you disagree with someone, state why but don't attack the person. You're trying to convince a majority of your peers to agree with you, not create enemies.

Discussion ends with a motion. A draft of the motion may be written for you, such as

I move to adopt/not adopt the new chewing gum regulations.

Please don't read the motion as drafted. It makes you sound stupid to say, "I move to adopt not adopt . . ." or "I move to approve or deny . . ." The voters pick up on your ignorance. Your choice is to pick one, or you can create your own motion, adding other items you feel necessary.

The chair asks for a second to the motion. If no second is received, the motion dies and a new motion is made. A substitute motion can also be made, which is a new motion to replace the initial one. The government body may or may not have rules about substitute motions.

After the motion is made and seconded, you discuss the motion. If you have something interesting to add, get recognized by the chair and make your statement. If you're voting against the motion, announce that you intend to do so and state why.

When discussion on the motion ends, you vote. You can vote via voice vote or roll call. For some topics, the law or policy may require that a roll call vote be made. It's tradition that any elected official can request a roll call vote.

Vote *aye* or *nay*, or you can say *yes* or *no*. Don't be cute and try to abstain, vote *present*, or ask to be passed over.

After the vote is taken, you do have an opportunity to change your vote. This parliamentary trick may apply in only a few situations — for example, you're distracted and you accidentally vote the wrong way. If so, after the vote is taken, immediately make an announcement that you'd like to change your vote.

After the vote is taken and recorded, the decision is made. My advice is never to grouse over it. If you've disagreed with what's passed, you must accept it as adopted policy. That's the way the system works.

>> The time limit for a second motion is at the discretion of the chair. I did see one public meeting on YouTube where a mayor held out for several minutes, waiting for a second. At that point, a council member should have offered a substitute motion.

>> Motions must be passed on agenda action items. If it's the body's desire not to adopt something or to skip an item, an appropriate dismissal motion must be made. The point is to keep a public record of all decisions.

>> Don't fret about being on the losing side of an issue. As long as you're keeping your campaign pledges, your supporters will be proud. Make a note of your defeat, which you can bring up should you run for reelection. Remind the voters that you tried.

REMEMBER

>> All your decisions have consequences for someone, though they may never affect you directly.

Chapter **19**

Your Reelection

O h, my! How the tables have turned. You began your political journey with perhaps the notion of "knocking off" an incumbent. And here you are, an elected official who seeks reelection. Time for someone else to knock off *you!*

The decision to run again is a natural one. Indeed, the reelection rate for local office is quite high, nearly 100 percent for some small districts. Some officials spend decades in office. Often, they run unopposed. These statistics, however, don't imply that, should you choose to run again, you'll stroll across the finish line on election day.

The Glory of Incumbency

Current officeholders have a tremendous advantage when it comes to an election. They claim that they're "defending their seat," though it's really the public's seat. And the defense isn't necessary unless they've done something untoward and everyone knows it. Most of the time, an incumbent is granted readmission to the same office.

Taking advantage of your advantage

Incumbents have an overwhelming advantage over challengers in every election. You may have already experienced this if you've run against an incumbent and lost. The incumbent advantage is one reason so many activists demand term limits.

Here are the advantages a current officeholder has over any challenger:

Name recognition: Folks who pay attention locally recognize your name. This isn't a huge number of people, but these are typically people of influence.

Reputation: Holding public office means you have a public record. Your votes on everything are recorded, as are your comments on certain issues. This material is better than a campaign promise because it's demonstrated and factual.

Ability to raise money: As a proven winner, individuals and businesses are more inclined to support you when asked.

Exposure in the press: Not only has your name appeared in the press, your position ads legitimacy to press releases and other campaign activities, making it more likely you see coverage.

People's reluctance toward change: Despite their incessant complaining about politics, most voters prefer to send the same people back to office time and time again.

The most important of these advantages is name recognition. It provides a huge advantage when it comes to running for office the first time or for reelection.

Understanding why voters keep incumbents

Stubborn voters need a damn good reason to remove an incumbent from office. Change requires a catalyst. For local office, this catalyst must be an issue that the voters are keenly aware of. Most of the time, however, such upset isn't to be found, which is why voters keep sending the same people back to office.

Voters are reluctant to toss out an incumbent unless the incumbent screwed up: They voted wrong on a popular issue. They mouthed off one too many times. They did something in their private life that was odious and well-publicized. Even with all this baggage, people may still vote for the incumbent, because they dislike the challenger more.

DAN SAYS

I confided in a candidate once that he had no chance to win his election. No, the only way for him to be victorious was for his incumbent opponent to lose. True to his calling, the incumbent perfectly executed a losing campaign: He publicly voiced disdain for the voters, bad-mouthed an employees' union, was frequently seen grumbling at public events, and once even told the crowd at a forum that he didn't need the job because he was already rich. Justifiably, he lost.

Reapplying for the same job

Your first reelection is the weakest. After that, it becomes increasingly difficult to vote out an incumbent. Though at some point in the future, long-toothed incumbents tend to become arrogant and therefore vulnerable.

The best way to have the public rehire you is to keep doing fine work. Showcase your strengths and accomplishments. Do the best job you can while in office and the voters will enjoy hiring you back.

REMEMBER

>> It's not your seat. They'll say it is: The press will say it — *everyone* says it. "Oh, you're running for Tim Anderson's seat?" But the seat belongs to the public. You're running for another term.

>> As a local officeholder, you're not a "full-time" politician. Yes, you technically are a politician, though a better term is *elected official*. Full-time politicians hold statewide or national office as a full-time job. They may start serving locally, but then they move on to become the truly terrible and despised full-time politicians.

>> Politicians who are elected officials aren't the only people practicing politics. You'll also find politics at your social club, church, school, community theater, hospital, or anywhere people get together. Politics is all over and sometimes it's nastier than the government type of politics.

Your Reelection Strategy

When you seek reelection, you build the same type of campaign you ran when you were first elected, though the theme is different: You want to keep the job. Just as you did before, you must gather a team, assemble lists, raise money, and create material for your reelection.

>> You might end up running unopposed, but don't get cocky. Plan your campaign regardless. Only after the filing deadline passes with no other opponents on the ballot can you back off and walk into office.

- The more opponents you have, the better your odds of winning reelection. This upsetting fact means that an unpopular incumbent draws lots of opposition, which means the unpopular incumbent generally wins anyway.

- Hopefully, you didn't use the word *elect* on your yard signs. If you didn't, you can reuse any you kept from your first campaign. See Chapter 12.

- You don't need to print business cards for your reelection. Instead, hand out your government business cards. Though you can't use government material for your campaign, the business cards are yours as an elected official. No restrictions are placed on whom you can give them to.

Touting your public record

Your campaign material for your reelection must detail your record in office. Demonstrate to the voters that you've kept your campaign promises, and promote any other items you accomplished. Hopefully, your record is strong and the public is familiar with your actions.

In addition to showcasing what you've done, pledge to make more accomplishments in the coming term. All elected officials have goals they'd like to see met; write them down.

Part of your insider advantage is that you're aware of some issues that a challenger may have no clue about. You've heard from the public as well as staff, so you can mention ongoing problems for which you have a solution. You can address what you see are the big oncoming issues with a relative degree of accuracy.

Opponents have a disadvantage because most don't research the organization as much as they should. It's easy for you to explain how a challenger's solution may not work. Better still, you can query a challenge about what research they've done to arrive at their conclusions.

The bottom line is that you come across as better informed as a candidate, which is just part of being an incumbent. Voters like knowledgeable, confident people.

Being an active candidate

One reason a long-term incumbent can lose an election is laziness. They don't put the energy into a campaign that an opponent is willing to devote. So they plant yard signs and send out a few tepid mailers, and that's about it. Meanwhile, an active opponent is knocking on doors and holding meet-and-greets all over the district. Such effort pays off, especially if the opponent is likable.

If you want to retain the job, you must work hard. The only time you get a pass is when your only opponent is on the ballot because "no one should run unopposed." If they don't campaign or even bother showing up to the forums, you're assured another term.

Term Limits

One of the political hot topics in the US is term limits, though the focus is primarily on Congress and not on local office. With the national government effectively dysfunctional and many Congress members serving for decades, term limits seem a logical solution for many frustrated people.

At the local level, the only true term limit is the term of office: You may be elected to a 2-, 3-, or 4-year term or longer. This limit by code is your term limit, because you must reapply for the same job if you want to continue serving.

Some jurisdictions may have further limits, such as only two or three consecutive terms in local office. But for the most part, with local office well off the radar of the angry mob, many officeholders enjoy multiple terms without much consternation.

You may also choose to term-limit yourself, which is a noble idea. If you plan on doing so, I offer two strong recommendations. First, announce your term limit at the start of your term. Second, stick with your pledge.

If you're going to start your last term in office, make the announcement during your campaign. Be public about it. "This will be my last term in office." There. Now stick with it.

> » Wags say that all politicians should have two terms: the first in office, the second in prison.

> » Our political system is designed for armatures to take office. If you meet the requirements to run for the office, you're good to go. Touting experience in holding office should count for nothing, though people boast about it as if somehow it mattered.

>> Avoiding self-imposed term limits is tough. First, you face pressure from supporters — and perhaps even government staff — if you're doing a good job. These people don't like change. Second, no politician comes equipped without an ego. If you term-limit yourself, don't let your bloated feeling of self-importance fool you into believing that somehow you're truly needed in office again.

DAN SAYS

>> I made the mistake of making a surprise announcement of my own term limits, which completely backfired. Quickly, I discovered that my desire not to run again was met by disbelief. Supporters as well as people I barely knew, informed me it was a bad idea. The problem was the surprise nature of my announcement. Truly, if you want to run "one last time," make that decision public when you campaign.

Groom a Replacement

One way to bow out of office gracefully is to find someone capable to replace you. This person need not be a perfect replacement (I mean, really!) but, rather, someone who can carry on your spirit and someone you're comfortable offering your public support.

To best groom a replacement, draft people you admire, or whom you'd like to see in public office, to serve on government committees. Encourage them to attend meetings. Guide them through the process. Offer them the kind of help you wish you'd had when you first ran for office.

If you can't find someone suitable, you can always endorse someone who's running. Such an endorsement carries great weight, but ensure that you're confident the person will hold true to their character. As I'm fond of saying, you never really know how anyone performs in office until they get into office. You don't want to ruin your own reputation by endorsing a dork.

By all means, if you can groom a replacement, do so. Endorse a candidate. But please do not resign so that an anointed successor takes the job. Such a tactic may benefit insiders and cronies, but it runs counter to the election process and is disrespectful to the voter.

RESIGN AND REPLACE

One thing I'd advise against is a slimy tactic used at small agencies — particularly, school districts. It's what I call the resign-and-replace anointment.

For example, you prefer not to run again, so you resign early. Seriously, unless you have some sort of emergency, or have moved from the district, you have no need to bail on the public. Yet, to keep the status quo, you resign a year or so before your term is up. Then the board is free to select a replacement, who is consistently someone who won't make waves, a go-along-get-along person.

Because the anointed replacement holds office, they run for reelection (their first election) as an incumbent. This advantage keeps them in office, which perpetuates the agency's groupthink and idea vitrification.

This resign-and-replace tactic was so bad at my local school district that for 15 years no trustee had initially taken office by winning an election; all of them were appointed after a resignation.

5

The Part of Tens

IN THIS PART . . .

Avoiding common campaign mistakes

Experiencing campaign highs and lows

Tolerating the elected-official experience

IN THIS CHAPTER

» **Funding shortages**

» **Blowing your money early**

» **Spending money foolishly**

» **Avoiding public events**

» **Mishandling campaign finances**

» **Abusing staff**

» **Engaging online trolls**

» **Ignoring your volunteer army**

» **Flubbing your facts**

» **Running a negative campaign**

Chapter **20**

Ten Common Campaign Mistakes

As you sift through morning rubble, you question what went wrong with your campaign. Chances are, you did a lot of things right. Perhaps you felt tremendously positive going into election night. Yet something didn't work; the voters chose someone else.

The flawless campaign doesn't exist. Mistakes happen. Some mistakes are minor and cause no trouble. Some major mistakes end up blowing over with no effects. Still other mistakes may not seem important, but they suffocate a campaign tried-and-true, especially when the victor took office by simply making fewer mistakes.

Not Raising Money

No campaign raises enough money, but losing campaigns fail to raise any money at all. The problem rests on the candidate's shoulders: It's your job to make the calls and bring in the funds. When you fail, your campaign runs underfunded, you lose marketing opportunities, and you lose the election.

>> I feel sad for the candidates who desire to be above money in politics, who decide to run for office and not fund-raise. The word for these individuals is clever: loser. No matter how noble you believe your effort, you must raise money if you plan to come in anything other than last on election night.

>> The key to making this mistake is in the word *raising*. It doesn't count when you completely self-fund your campaign. Higher offices can be bought by millionaires, but local office is won by wide support. A fully self-funded campaign sends a message that you don't have wide support.

>> The secret to raising money is to ask. See Chapter 11 for details on campaign financing.

Spending Money Early

Some first-time candidates are so excited to be in an election: They have money, and they're cocky about their chances, so they decide to market themselves early: Eight weeks before election day, they blast out a mailer to all voters in the district. Take that, everyone else!

Well, everyone else is probably laughing. Such a huge marketing push may work when you open a dry-cleaning store, but for an election campaign, the closer you can deliver material to election day, the better.

After blowing all your money early, you have less to spend during the final, critical weeks of the campaign. This time is when the serious candidates are sending out their marketing material. The stuff you sent out weeks earlier? It's already been recycled — probably into the new campaign fliers sent out by your opponents. Smart move.

Misspending Money

When you file for office, you see a new type of junk mail appear. It consists of advertisements for campaign swag: hats, pins, bumper stickers, Frisbees, pencils, and all sorts of jolly, festive stuff that only a fool would buy.

If your campaign budget is overflowing with money, which it isn't, consider buying some swag and sharing it with your supporters. They'll love it! The effectiveness of such junk getting you into local office is dubious.

Campaign money is precious. Your priority in spending it is to connect with voters — specifically, chronic do-or-die voters. (Refer to Chapter 7 for details on identifying chronic voters.) The best way to communicate with them is by direct mail, door-knocking, phoning, and other chores that don't involve festive buttons or silly hats.

Seriously, no one has ever looked at a campaign hat and said, "Hey! Now I know who to vote for."

Not Showing Up

Your campaign is your full-time job, but it's also a job application. As with anyone applying for a job, showing up is 90 percent of the effort.

Ensure that you always show up to campaign events. Don't make a lame excuse. If you believe that the event is hosted by a hostile entity, show up anyway. Being in office doesn't shield you from hostility, so you'd better prepare now.

If you're not invited to an event, show up anyway — providing the event is open to the public. Don't be disruptive; you need not make a scene or pound your shoe on the table. People will notice that you showed up. Your opponents who showed up will be uncomfortable. That's all you need to do.

Not Tracking Finances

Don't ever be sloppy with campaign money. The campaign is a business, and you must track revenue and expenses just as diligently as any small-business owner. Further, you may be required to report your finances during the campaign. Being accurate and honest is vital.

>> If you're bad with money, appoint someone else to run the finances. Even when you're good with money, having someone else check the income and expenses means one less thing for you to do.

>> No, you don't want to let anyone know that you're bad with money. They'll find out soon enough should the voters make a mistake and put you into office.

Mistreating Staff and Supporters

Running for local office the first time doesn't endow you with the haughtiness of a multi-decade United States senator who can afford to be arrogant and rude and treat people with disdain. Still, some candidates think that by virtue of having their name on the ballot, they become someone become morally and intellectually superior to everyone else.

Always respect your campaign staff, who are volunteers. They work because they like you. Giving them praise and thanks is vital to this relationship.

Don't ditch out on a fundraiser or meet-and-greet. Be the first one there. Say hello to everyone. Spend time with as many people as possible. You may not be the host, but you're the main attraction. Even if you hate crowds, pretend that you're enjoying yourself. It's expected.

WARNING

When the campaign screws up (and it will), do not blame underlings for mistakes. All mistakes are yours; you own them. A candidate who blames "staff" or "miscommunication" for a gaffe, especially one that's reported in the press, comes across as slimy. Own your problems.

Arguing with Idiots Online

Don't bother trying to figure out the motives of an Internet troll. They thrive during campaign season, hiding under a blanket of anonymity, eager to see a candidate take a misstep. The temptation to engage them is great, but only a fool would fall into their traps.

To avoid the Internet troll, as well as the usual idiots who support your opponent or just hate you for whatever reason, I offer the following advice tidbits:

Stay the hell offline during the campaign. This approach is probably best. Yes, it's difficult to wean yourself from the social network teat. If you can stay online but not engage anyone, the results work out positively for you.

Stick to your own issues on Facebook and Twitter. If you must use social media during the campaign, do so on your own terms. Make your own posts. Reply to legitimate questions. Do not engage the trolls.

Respond to attacks with facts incidentally presented. If you must, ensure that when you address an issue, you do so with facts, such as names, dates, and so on. The goal is to respond only once; never get into a conversation with an anonymous online jerk who has no interest in promoting your campaign.

Let your volunteers get into the mud. A great way to put your volunteer army to work is to let them wrestle with the pigs. Have them go at it, attack, rebut, sling the mud. Their interaction will help your bruised ego as well as disengage you from direct combat.

One tactic to take, which I've used successfully even as an elected official, is to reply to any online jerk with the following: "I would love to address this issue with you personally. Please reach out to my email or phone me. Let's discuss." Of course, you put your email and phone number in the message.

In all the times I've directly confronted trolls with my email address or phone number, not one has bothered to contact me. Generally, my post is the last in the thread.

Not Using Volunteers

Your best resource costs you the least amount of money (free) and generates the best results. Your volunteers are eager to help your campaign and to do amazing things for you — if you ask.

>> Whenever you're faced with a big task, phone your volunteers and ask who can help.

>> Don't be disappointed if a volunteer can't make it. Just keep calling. Better, ask them for ideas on how they can help.

>> Invite your volunteers to meet-and-greets and other fundraisers. You should take pictures of the huge crowds at these events and post them to social media. Your opponents will take notice.

» As with anyone else, it helps to inform your volunteers of events well in advance. Ensure that you remind them of upcoming events, such as a neighborhood canvas, a phone bank, an envelope-stuffing party, and so on. The further in advance you can let them know what's going on, the better their attendance.

Getting Facts Wrong

The worst campaign mistake is the one you make yourself. Stepping on your tongue is something you want to avoid. It may not be a major mistake, but it's something your opponent can play with for a while.

For example, you claim the budget has increased by 20 percent a year for the past five years. Your numbers are off. You're taken to task for the misquote — and rightly so. "If Tim Anderson can't get his budget percentages correct at this point, imagine how terrible he'll be if elected."

The best way to avoid gaffes is to make your point nonspecifically. Say, "The budget has increased dramatically for the past five years." In fact, this statement is true for any government agency, because few of them shrink.

» Generalize, but don't be vague.

» Especially in debates, give a range of values or a "greater than" value instead of quoting specific numbers.

**DAN
SAYS**

» I know a candidate who was endlessly harangued because she was off by $100 in a quote. Her number was close enough, and her error was less than one-tenth of a percent, but her opponents disliked her so much that they rode that thin horse all the way to election day.

Going Negative

Everyone wants to run a positive campaign. You want to tout your virtues and trust that the public agrees and sends you into office. Going negative, where you attack your opponent — fairly or unfairly — is seen as a sign of weakness. And truly, such campaigning rarely changes anyone's mind.

The concept of going negative is a spectrum. Its definition varies. Obviously, your opponent may think a piece that exposes his public record is "antagonistic mudslinging," but it isn't. And, of course, personal attacks and fabrications are examples of serious negative campaigning.

Where going negative hurts you the most is when it's done early. Your first campaign pieces are introductions. They must be positive. If you must run a comparison piece, or decide to openly attack an opponent for some legitimate reason, hold the material for later. Or, if you feel you're doing well, hold it forever.

REMEMBER

>> Your opponent's reaction to any of your campaign material as negative or "mudslinging" shows how afraid they are more than it shows whether you've truly gone negative.

>> Everyone takes things personally in a political campaign.

>> See Chapter 12 for more details on the consequences of going negative.

Chapter **21**

Ten Ups and Downs

The campaign emotional rollercoaster is like no other ride in the amusement park of life. You will experience tremendous highs. You will suffer painful lows. You'll stare at yourself blankly in the bathroom mirror and question why you put yourself through such an ordeal. These ups and downs are fleeting and to be expected.

Up and Down: Polls

Local-office candidates rarely have money to do polling — and I mean legitimate, professional polling. Expect to pay tens of thousands of dollars for such a thing. The close substitute is the online poll, which is statistically meaningless, but every candidate I know lamentably takes them seriously.

When you see your name atop the polls, you rejoice. When you trail in the polls, your spirit sinks. It's all nonsense, of course: The only poll that matters is the election.

>> Online polls are manipulated. Don't take them seriously.

>> Don't be misled by casual polling data, either. Just because everyone you meet at the farmer's market is supportive is no reflection of how actual voters feel.

>> If someone does do professional polling, the results can be considered accurate — for the timeframe. Changes during the campaign can affect polling data. The margin of error is also important: When two candidates are close in a professional poll, the race can go either way.

Up: Money Comes In

Nothing is more satisfying than receiving some campaign funds, even if the checks were expected. Opening envelopes after a meet-and-greet is like opening presents Christmas morning. Having a supporter approach you and hand you an envelope is also thrilling, especially when it's a thick envelope and you hope no one is taking a candid photo.

>> Money comes in best when you ask for it. If the money isn't coming in, and you want it to, see Chapter 11.

>> The high you receive along with the campaign contribution is fleeting. Rarely will you have enough money to do the things you need.

Down: Press Coverage

Depending on the size of the district, and the presence of local media in your area, you may not see any press coverage for your campaign. Perhaps the only time you see your name is when you announce. After that, blissful silence.

For a higher-profile local race, you may see your name in the paper quite often, though the frequency really depends on the campaign and whether the press thinks your race is interesting. An article about your campaign won't be a surprise; you know it's coming, because a reporter has contacted you and taken quotes.

Reading the article will most likely be a downer for you. That's because you forget that the press isn't taking a side. In fact, your supporters may phone to complain about the biased interview and how it favors your opponent. Such perception is common.

Regardless of how you feel, understand that press coverage is good. Any mention at all in the paper shows that you're running a legitimate campaign and the media is taking you seriously. Forget that the reporter wasn't singing your praises or unduly slamming your opponent.

>> Your local paper may choose not to endorse candidates for local office, especially for smaller districts. Don't be disappointed! Even when the paper does endorse, the effects on the election outcome are dubious; local newspapers tend to support the status quo unless some burning issue has ticked off the editor. In this instance, editorials leading up to the election let you know where the paper stands.

DAN SAYS

>> I thought an article about my most recent election was fair, but my supporters called me in droves complaining that it was biased. So I read the piece again and I could see what they were saying, but again the piece didn't praise my opponent, either.

>> Refer to Chapter 16 for tips on dealing with the press.

Up: Unexpected Support

Nothing brightens your day like an unexpected check in the mail, letter to the editor, or sign of support from a strong quarter. Such a pick-me-up is welcome, and frequently happens at a time where you most need a boost.

The reason an unanticipated donation is so uplifting is that it's quite rare. As you may already know, getting money from your most ardent supporters requires a phone call or in-person visit. So when you receive an unsolicited check or online donation, it's heartening.

It's a common campaign tactic to get your supporters and volunteers to write letters to the editor. But it makes you smile when you see an unexpected letter of support.

Getting an unexpected and welcome endorsement is also a high. It speaks strongly when a respected civic leader steps up to the plate and sings your praises without any overtures on your part. Of course, no one knows it's unexpected, but it still counts as a high.

>> Unexpected support can also come from people who phone you out of the blue. They may ask for a yard sign or volunteer to host a meet-and-greet.

>> Just as you may receive an unexpected letter of support in the paper, you'll also see letters from people you thought might support you who instead support your opponent.

Down: Your Opponent is Doing Well

It may seem like your opponent is always doing well, which affects your emotional state. Still, such an observation has little to do with the outcome of the election. If you let it affect you emotionally, however, and you come across as miserable in public, the voters will notice.

Examples of your opponent doing well include endorsements by civic leaders — especially if you sought out the same endorsements — receiving large checks, huge leads in polling, great attendance at rallies, and other disheartening evidence that may lead you to believe yours is a lost cause.

Your opinion of your opponent doing well is subjective, of course. The only concern you should have is how it affects you in public. Remember, Americans love an underdog. If so, position yourself that way.

Up: You See an Effect

A subtle thing you may not notice is how your campaign is affecting the tone of the election. What to look for are issues you've raised that are quickly being addressed or even adopted by your opponents.

For example, one of your issues may be paying attention to a specific part of town. You mention it in your literature, but opponents don't touch upon it. Eventually, you see other candidates addressing those issues. This change means you're having an effect.

>> It's tough to find an issue that resonates with the voters, especially for those off-the-radar elected positions. When you see an effect, it means that you've truly done your homework. Congratulations.

>> Having an effect is often the best outcome for many candidates. Raising issues and drawing them into focus keeps the other candidates in line, especially when they see the public react positively after the issues are addressed.

Down: Stress

The campaign season is plagued with periods of stress. Expect it. Stress happens to all candidates, even the cocky incumbents who seemingly walk to victory while twirling a cane.

Aspects of stress include anxiety attacks and irregular sleep patterns. You may experience such events even when you think you're doing well.

One of the big issues is that it's difficult not to take the campaign personally. Even those politicians with thick skin are affected by nasty things people say. The point is not to let it appear to bother you: Stay positive and keep moving forward.

Up: Positive Feedback

Don't ignore your supporters and volunteers when they compliment you. This positive feedback must be appreciated. Thank them for it.

It's easy to overlook positive feedback when you're at the center of the campaign cyclone. You see the data, know the financials, and anticipate the tremendous amount of work yet to do. When a supporter calls and mentions how great they think you're doing, take heart.

Consider positive feedback as you schedule events, fundraisers, and meet-and-greets. Nothing lifts your spirits like seeing people eager to support you. Such events provide an emotional boost late in the campaign.

Down: No-Shows

It happens to every candidate: You schedule an event and few people show up. In fact, your campaign staff may outnumber the regular people in attendance.

No-shows happen at all levels of politics. Just as candidates love to show photos of rooms packed with reporters and overflowing crowds, they taunt their opponents with images of unmotivated groups of people glumly standing around an empty hall. Indeed, it happens to everyone.

DAN SAYS

My advice is to press on. I once had a wonderful lady throw me a meet-and-greet with a fabulous spread. She was famous for these events, and I was certain her home would be filled with neighbors. Only two showed up. Still, I did my best.

Up: You Did It

It's a rare accomplishment that someone runs for office. True, some may do it only once and they're done. Yet it's an amazing thing to experience, to see how the process works and to play a role in the Republic.

Win or lose, good campaign or bad, you will eventually feel contentment after the process is done. Be proud.

» Letting the staff decide

» Patting yourself on the back

» Showing respect

» Being underinformed

» Punting decisions

» Dealing with lazy peers

» Draining the energy level

» Suffering through subcommittees

» Ignoring the experts

Chapter **22**

Ten Frustrations of an Elected Official

Sure, everyone wants to be Lord High Ruler of a local government body. Imagine the things you could accomplish! Then again, such a position didn't work out well for Julius Caesar. You might end up with the same fate, though being stabbed to death by your fellow Library District Commissioners might not make the history books.

Government runs slowly. Even the most sensical, logical policies take years to develop. You can passionately implore your fellow elected officials to make a wise choice. You find the public overwhelmingly on your side, yet nothing seems to get done. This is how the system works. It's much better than dictatorship, but it isn't without its frustrations.

Staff Offers Yes–No "Decisions"

The myth is that the members of an elected board are the decision-makers for the organization. The reality is, most of the time, they're a rubber stamp. That's because the decisions are presented as yes-or-no.

Such a vote informs you that staff, or a subcommittee, has already made the decision. They've reviewed the options, peeled away what they believe won't work, and come up with a final recommendation for a Colosseum-like thumbs-up or thumbs-down from the elected officials. Pretty much all the time they get a thumbs-up, which is what the bureaucrats want. So why is staff running the outfit?

If an elected board is truly in charge, staff presents options: "Here are the top three choices for the new library. Location A is preferred by Library Staff, Location B is the least expensive, and Location C is desired by the public." Then let the board debate — in public — regarding which location to choose. All too often, and disappointingly, the board is presented with Location A as the best, yes-or-no, do-or-die.

The preselected choice is even more obnoxious because if the board objects, staff whines about all the "work" they put into the choice; they bemoan that it will be difficult and expensive to unwind the clock. This threat is designed to intimidate the elected officials into rubber-stamping the only option given. Nearly all the time, it works.

DAN SAYS

Don't let unelected staff rob the public of a choice!

Electeds Kowtow to Staff

Staff has a job to present issues to an elected body, upon which the board makes the final decision. It's your job as an elected official to review the material. You cast a vote based on what you think is best for the people or the organization. Often, the decision is easy.

What's annoying, however, is when an elected official dithers. I've seen this happen several times: A board member is conflicted over which way to vote. So they ask staff, "What would you do?"

You would think that, after suffering through a campaign and an election, someone holding office would be honored to make their own decision. Still, the occasional elected official kowtows to staff for help.

Fortunately, most staff differ on the question. I've seen staffers say outright, "This is not my decision to make. You've heard my report." Even then, some electeds press the matter. I find it annoying and frustrating to watch.

Any elected board is going to have nonthinkers as members. After all, you need a name, not a brain, to win an election. Many voters fail to see the stupidity of an elected official asking an unelected staff member how they would vote on something. And these people keep getting elected.

You were elected to make your own decisions. Get input from staff, but never use them as a crutch to justify your vote.

DAN SAYS

Electeds Keep Congratulating Staff

Local government involves a lot of back-slapping. This monstrous aberration would never happen in the corporate world.

Consider a board meeting of some major corporation:

COMMITTEE CHAIR: Board, we just completed that report you asked for. Sorry that it's a month late. Still, I believe you'll be pleased with the results.

BOARD MEMBER: Thank you for all your hard work on doing the task you were assigned to do. We really appreciate the long hours and tireless effort you put into crafting a masterful report — possibly, the best one produced.

Such a thing is nonsense in the corporate world, but common in government. Workers are routinely praised and given high regard for doing the job they're paid to do. Yes, Bill's team poured the concrete walkway. Ta-da! They got paid, right? That's all the praise required. But in government, elected officials routinely break down and congratulate workers for doing their jobs.

I'm not trying to invalidate the jobs done by government employees. Many of them do outstanding work and truly serve the public. Only in government, however, do elected officials congratulate someone for doing the task that's expected of them or, disappointingly, the bare minimum.

>> The worst offense seems to happen at budget time, when an elected thanks the financial officer or treasurer for preparing the budget. Duh. That's their job.

>> Above-and-beyond effort should be recognized, of course. But when the board routinely commends someone who does the job they're paid to do, those extra efforts lose meaning.

DAN SAYS

The Whole "Sir" Thing

Being polite is an excellent attribute. Referring to people by their title shows respect. So don't be taken aback when staff members refer to you as *sir* or *ma'am* or by your elected title. Even if you're a doofus and they know it, staff shows respect.

If you prefer more casual communications, you can always ask. Still, don't be offended or taken aback when you're consistently addressed in a formal manner.

Also, be on the lookout for someone who pours on the titles a bit thick. I'm okay with showing respect, but obvious ass-kissing tingles my Spidey sense that someone desires me to look the other way.

I'm not a fan of being called Sir or addressed formally. Yet I figure the staffer is most likely referring to my position and the public I represent as opposed to me personally. Don't let polite behavior toward you as an elected official go to your head.

DAN SAYS

Out of the Loop

You must be an informed elected official in order to do the best job possible. Beyond reading the material you're given, go above and beyond to seek out more information: Meet with department heads and division chiefs, visit with the people who do the work, interact with the public. Overflow yourself with information.

Despite the best efforts of staff, however, you will occasionally find yourself outside of the loop. Especially in a larger organization, don't be surprised when you're the last one to know.

JUNIOR HIGH SCHOOL POLITICS

Sometimes, keeping elected officials out of the loop is done on purpose. It's what I call "junior high school politics," and it happens frequently to newly elected officials who won by running against the status quo. Don't let such reindeer games bother you. Instead, work to keep yourself informed.

When you're certain that other elected officials are withholding information, bring up the issue at the public meeting. Don't be accusatory — be interrogative. Ask them, "In what manner is the entire body being informed?" Or if it's obvious that some elected officials are more equal than others, mention it as an aside: "It would be beneficial to the public if all trustees were informed at the same level regarding this topic." You can point out to the public that other officials are being immature without looking immature yourself.

An example of being out of the loop is when you read in the paper about something your agency is doing — about which you had no idea. Worse is when a reporter or citizen phones and asks you about some impending event and you know nothing about it.

Most agencies strive to keep elected officials informed. At the local level, however, elected officials are part-time. It's easy for the agency to get wound up in something and, disappointingly, assume that the elected officials all know. Rarely is it the intention of staff to drop the ball.

DAN SAYS

It's perfectly acceptable to confront staff when you feel underinformed. Do so in person. Do not raise the issue in an email or at a public meeting. You have every right to be upset.

Someone Punts

Some decisions percolate to the board level that have no business rising so far. After all, the function of an agency's policy is to guide decisions. This process makes it possible for the government to run without an elected body present and voting at all times.

When staff is unwilling to follow the guidelines, they often bring the issue to the elected body. Such a move is obvious to a seasoned elected official: Staff is uncomfortable. They don't clearly state the reasons why the issue is coming to the board. They offer conflicting statements.

You may never know the reason the issue is being brought forward, which is a process I call *punting*. As in football, when the team runs out of plays and cannot score, they kick away the ball. Staff does this as well as subcommittees when faced with an issue that may be too political for their comfort level.

DAN SAYS

My approach to the occasional punt is to move to direct staff or the committee to follow the written policy. If they have an issue with this solution, they'll tell you, and it may explain a lot. For example, the policy would anger a popular local businessman and staff is fearful. Seriously, such a thing happens all the time.

In the bigger picture, a punt indicates that an item may need more work. Move to schedule a workshop so that the item can be fully vetted.

When Peers Are Obviously Unprepared

No rule states than an elected official must be prepared, ever. Many make careers of showing up without reading the packet or even knowing what's going on. Amazingly, you can spot such officials if you watch the meeting. It's something to behold.

The good news is that anyone who can win an election can easily fake their way around being informed in a public meeting. The first and best tactic is to keep your mouth shut. Sit and watch, then vote. No one is the wiser.

Worse is when an elected official's ego cup overflows and they feel they must contribute something substantial to demonstrate how learned they are. Odds are long, but they might pull it off. After all, even a blind squirrel occasionally finds a nut. Still, most of the time, the official comes off looking like a fool, which is quite entertaining.

DAN SAYS

It would be brilliant if everyone showed up to the meeting fully prepared and eager to take on the public's business. Consider yourself blessed if that's the case. Otherwise, you must endure your fellow elected official's weaknesses.

People Who Suck the Air Out of the Room

In a campaign forum, candidates are given a time allotment in which to respond. Whether it's 1 minute, 2 minutes, or 5 minutes, the candidate fills the span with words, words, words. Politicians love to talk.

The problem with an elected official given reign to talk is that they can take an immeasurable amount of time in which to do so. I doubt that I've ever been to any public meeting where the phrase "Get to the point" hasn't rattled around in my head a dozen times. I refer to such bloviation as sucking the air from the room. It truly does lower the energy level.

Spewing an endless string of words that say little isn't confined to the role of an elected official's mouth. Often, you'll encounter staff and hired experts who make presentations at a speed one notch above stop:

This. Is. Our. Annual. Report. On. Growth. In. The. Southern. Part. Of. Our. District.

It's maddening!

Especially if you're in education, be prepared for lots of feather-light words that flow at molten lava speed. Offering information one teaspoon as a time seems to be the standard for any educational presentation.

DAN SAYS

No one put a gun to your head and told you to run for public office. People whose train of thought rambles the way a football bounces must be tolerated. Try not to roll your eyes or make dramatic gestures to demonstrate how bored you are. Just put up with it.

Subcommittee Overload

Subcommittees offer a chance for a variety of citizens and experts to provide input and feedback, greatly enhancing the information flow for the elected official. At the same time, subcommittees can be so dreadful that it's common in government to refer to them as "the S-word."

Here are some ways a subcommittee can become counterproductive:

Vitrified committees: It's common for committees to recommend their own members. This happens because either the agency does a poor job of communicating position openings or few members of the public want to be involved. Either way, when the committee keeps picking its own members, they devolve into like-minded groupthink. The committee vitrifies and follows the adage, "We've always done it this way." It's at that point I'd prefer the entire committee be dissolved and replaced.

Stacked committees: It's common for some elected officials who don't trust the public to stack a citizen's subcommittee with staff and other elected officials. I always check the committee roster to see how many members are from the general public versus how many are paid staffers or elected officials. Even from the general public, certain "stakeholders" may be preselected — usually, comfortable yes votes for the status quo. If you want honest feedback from a committee, ensure that it's not stacked.

Committee overload: Subcommittees that spawn subcommittees run the risk of stopping all action. For each committee, a meeting must be held. Form a subcommittee and you're guaranteed several meetings just to get the subcommittee up and running, let alone complete its task. Avoid having too many subcommittees and sub-subcommittees and an overabundance of meetings.

Mission creep: When a committee runs out of things to do, it invents new tasks for itself. This process happens slowly. The new tasks are related to the original mission statement but expand its definition broadly. If left unchecked, eventually the subcommittee seeks out more power and can become belligerent. As an elected official, read the subcommittee meeting minutes to ensure that mission creep isn't taking hold. If you think it is, mention it to administration.

Overthinking the politics: I've sat in on a committee meeting once (before I was elected) and heard a member say, "I don't think the elected officials will go for this." After a discussion, the idea was dropped, which is tremendously sad. The point of the committee is to get opinions beyond those of the elected officials. Certainly, they may disagree, but the different opinions deserve to be heard.

I am a fan of the subcommittee structure and appreciate the feedback that comes from the committees. The system works well, providing the committees keep their focus.

» Government subcommittees are subject to the same levels of transparency as the parent organization. This rule means meetings must be scheduled with a published agenda and open to the public. Subcommittee documents may also be available to the public.

» If you create an ad hoc committee, which is a committee with a single, limited purpose, ensure that it has an expiration date. That can be a date certain or after a project is completed. Like any committee, an ad hoc committee can fall victim to many of the committee problems mentioned in this section. It's best to keep such a committee focused and then thank and dismiss them when the work is complete.

DAN SAYS

>> The worst example of committee-stacking I've seen is one committee where only 2 of the 21 members could be considered from the general public. The rest were a mix of paid staff, hand-picked stakeholders, and elected officials. Needless to say, the committee's decisions always agreed with the power players.

Experts to Ignore

Government hires a lot of outside experts, consultants, and contractors. These professionals offer expertise beyond what staff is capable of. Many of their duties are routine, important parts of the agency's work. Occasionally, a specialist or consultant is hired to work on a specific report.

For example, a city may hire a consultant to do a parking study, which confirms where more parking is needed. A water district may hire a consultant to confirm whether fees are set properly. Experts are hired to do the research, write the report, and then present it to the elected body.

Rarely have I seen any expert report come back that didn't agree with assumptions already made. For example, the water district wants to raise its rates. They hire the consultant who invariably agrees with them. That's the essence of these reports — which may be required by law but generally agree with whatever consensus the agency has already established.

Regardless of the report's outcome, the elected body may ignore the expert opinion. This refute rarely happens to those reports claiming to raise fees. Instead, elected officials ignore an expert opinion whenever it fails to jibe with their political desires.

For example, the report says the parking situation is just fine and the fees are adequate. This expert conclusion doesn't mirror the city council's political sentiments, so the report is ignored: Fees are increased and new parking lots built.

DAN SAYS

As an elected official, it's your choice to agree with the experts and consultants. Many of them hold the understanding that the board will rubber-stamp their recommendation. Ensure that's not always the case; make the expert work for it.

>> If you research your local government, you'll find lots of reports sitting on shelves. They're marvelous to investigate. Nothing makes you feel good as an elected official like quoting an old report that the body has previously adopted and ignored.

>> Raising rates or fees just because your district doesn't charge as much as surrounding districts is nonsense. Fees pay for services. If the fees are paying for services already, they need not be raised.

>> If you're skeptical that the hired consultant will merely echo the sentiments of staff, ask to be placed on the consultant selection committee. Review the submitted proposals to see how frequently a consultant comes to a preordained solution.

>> Many government consultants are former government employees. They know how the system works and how to get an inside edge.

>> No matter how tight the budget, it seems that the government always has money to hire a consultant.

Index

About the Author

Dan Gookin works full time as a technology author and online instructor. He's written over 160 titles on computers and high-tech, including *DOS For Dummies*, which founded the entire *For Dummies* brand. His part-time job is in government, where he's nearing the end of his second term on the city council in Coeur d'Alene, Idaho.

On a lark, in 2002 Dan ran as a Libertarian for the Idaho State Senate. He came in third in a two-way race; the Democratic challenger dropped out of the race, but still garnered more votes. Willing to make a difference, Dan began exploring local politics on a serious level. He applied his skills from high-tech to determine how problems could be solved and the people best served.

In 2007, he ran for the Coeur d'Alene city council against a favorite, long-term incumbent yet won 47 percent of the vote. Dan ran again in 2009 but lost with 49.5 percent of the vote. Ready to toss in the towel, he discovered that the then-mayor and council were non-transparently pushing a major park renovation without a public vote. In 2011, Dan ran for council a third time. He won a 5-way race with 53 percent of the vote. In 2015, he won reelection while running unopposed.

Dan has been registered as a Libertarian, a Republican, and an Independent. He's disappointed by the bitterness and division of national partisan politics, preferring to look at all angles for the best solution. Philosophically, he is a fiscally conservative yet socially liberal politician who believes his first duty as an elected official is to protect your rights.

Publisher's Acknowledgments

Acquisitions Editor: Lindsay Lefevere
Senior Project Editor: Paul Levesque
Copy Editor: Becky Whitney
Editorial Assistant: Matthew Lowe
Sr. Editorial Assistant: Cherie Case

Production Editor: Magesh Elangovan
Cover Image: © BackyardProduction/ Getty Images

Take dummies with you everywhere you go!

Whether you are excited about e-books, want more from the web, must have your mobile apps, or are swept up in social media, dummies makes everything easier.

Find us online!

dummies.com

dummies®
A Wiley Brand

Dummies is the global leader in the reference category and one of the most trusted and highly regarded brands in the world. No longer just focused on books, customers now have access to the dummies content they need in the format they want. Together we'll craft a solution that engages your customers, stands out from the competition, and helps you meet your goals.

Advertising & Sponsorships

Connect with an engaged audience on a powerful multimedia site, and position your message alongside expert how-to content. Dummies.com is a one-stop shop for free, online information and know-how curated by a team of experts.

- Targeted ads
- Video
- Email Marketing
- Microsites
- Sweepstakes sponsorship

20 MILLION PAGE VIEWS EVERY SINGLE MONTH

15 MILLION UNIQUE VISITORS PER MONTH

43% OF ALL VISITORS ACCESS THE SITE VIA THEIR MOBILE DEVICES

700,000 NEWSLETTER SUBSCRIPTION TO THE INBOXES OF
300,000 UNIQUE INDIVIDUALS EVERY WEEK

# of dummies

Custom Publishing

Reach a global audience in any language by creating a solution that will differentiate you from competitors, amplify your message, and encourage customers to make a buying decision.

- Apps
- Books
- eBooks
- Video
- Audio
- Webinars

Brand Licensing & Content

Leverage the strength of the world's most popular reference brand to reach new audiences and channels of distribution.

For more information, visit dummies.com/biz

    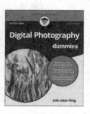

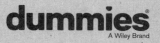